PSALMS

PSALMS

Introduced by
DAVID ADAM

DARTON·LONGMAN+TODD

This edition of the Book of Psalms first published in 2010 by
Darton, Longman and Todd Ltd
1 Spencer Court
140-142 Wandsworth High Street
London SW18 4JJ

Biblical text © 1985 by Darton, Longman and Todd Ltd and Doubleday,
an imprint of the Doubleday Publishing Group, a division of Random
House, Inc., New York

Nihil obstat Anthony Cowan
Imprimatur Rt Rev John Crowley V. G. Bishop in Central London
Westminster 4th September 1989

The Nihil obstat *and* Imprimatur *are a declaration that a book or pamphlet is
considered to be free from doctrinal or moral error. It is not implied that those who
have granted the Nihil obstat and Imprimatur agree with the contents, opinions or
statements expressed.*

Editions of the New Jerusalem Bible published by Darton, Longman
and Todd are NOT TO BE SOLD TO OR IN USA, Canada or the
Philippine Republic. For these territories the New Jerusalem Bible is
published by Doubleday, New York.

ISBN 978-0-232-52804-6

A catalogue record for this book is available from the British Library.

Produced by Judy Linard
Printed and bound in Great Britain by Thomson Litho, East Kilbride,
Scotland

INTRODUCTION

David Adam

The Book of Psalms is the largest book in the Bible, the most quoted book of the Old Testament in the New Testament and some of the Psalms are the most read literature in the world.

Once, I could say I knew most of its 'chapters' off by heart: by heart, rather than by memory alone, for I learnt them in worship. Sometimes I would read them quietly and meditate upon them; other times I would sing them in Gregorian or Anglican chant. Often I said them as part of one of two groups saying them antiphonally (that is, saying verse and verse about). I can say I have read part of this book every day for over fifty years, and have usually read most of it through every month. I am still learning from it, and being enriched by it, and so I commend it to you.

I can remember attending a church service high on the moors. Outside the scenery was glorious and the day bright. Inside the church it was cold, the books smelt musty and there was green mould creeping up some of the walls. The person who was taking the service was far from inspiring and it would have been easy to be put off. But there in this church, painted above the east window, was a wonderful message from Psalm 95: 'Let us come before his presence with thanksgiving: and show ourselves glad in him with psalms.' I was not there to pass judgement on my surroundings: I was there to give thanks to the ever present God and praise him in Psalms. The directions from this verse transformed the whole of what I was seeking to do, and still do today.

On another occasion I was asked to visit an elderly lady who was dying. My vicar sent me because he found the woman cantankerous! I, a young curate, arrogantly prepared to 'take God' to this lady. When I was shown into her room she asked me to sit down. She said: 'Let us say some psalms together.' There were no books but fortunately I had been saying the Psalms for a few years by then. We said them, verse and verse about, and she chose her favourites. In her frail voice she recited Psalms 23, 95, 100, 103, 121 and 148, and then asked for a blessing. I gave the blessing with tears in my eyes. I foolishly had thought I was taking God to her, and discovered he had been there long before me! I also received a great lesson in the importance of knowing prayers that you love off by heart. That in a time of trouble or dryness they can be a great strength. My own mother said the Psalter through each month during the long time she was ill. When my mother died my sister 'inherited' her prayer book and continued with the Psalm-saying for many years until her own death.

The Psalms are the Bible's own song book and encourage us to lift up our hearts to God. The word 'psalm' is from the Greek word 'psalmos', simply meaning song. The word does not have a special religious connotation, for the Jewish people thought of all of life relating to God and not just the part of it which we would call religious. Similarly, our belief in God should show in our attitude to all of his creation. These songs have arisen out of every phase of life: out of joy and sorrow, out of success and failure. They were sung in times of prosperity and times of persecution, war and exile.

The Psalms speak to the human condition and for this reason are still the most widely read portion of Old Testament today. They are used by most denominations within the Christian Church as well as by the Jews. They have often been printed and bound together with the Gospels. Their message goes through the whole spectrum of human life, from the depths of despair and dereliction to the heights of joy and praise. They express vitality for life in all its ups and downs, in the presence and seeming absence of God.

The Psalms are not formal statements of doctrine but poetry, intended to be set to music. The Hebrew people understood well the power of verse and music as a means to express their deepest feelings and experiences. As the hymnbook of the Jews, Psalms contains songs stretching over hundreds of years. The dating of individual psalms is difficult, though some of them are now about 3,000 years old, dating back to 1000BC, the time of King David. It is wonderful to think that some are songs from the Bronze Age and can still speak to us today.

There is a saying in Judaism: 'As Moses gave us the Pentateuch (that is, the first five books of the Bible) David gave the five books of the Psalms.' David is traditionally seen as the author of most of the psalms. Yet, if you read the headings to some of the psalms, you will discover some are written by other than David. For instance the entire third book, Psalms 73-89, is attributed others: Asaph wrote Psalms 73-83, Korah wrote 84-88 and Ethan the Ezrahite wrote 89. Some psalms were written well after David's time: a good example is Psalm 139, which was composed during the Babylonian Captivity (586-539BC). The longest psalm is the 119th and it probably comes after the Temple has been rebuilt (515BC). In the division into its five books, Book One (Psalms 1-41) and Book Two (Psalms 42-72) generally speaking seem to concentrate on the earliest period in the days of King David and Solomon. Book Three (Psalms 73-89), Book Four (Psalms 90-106) and Book Five (Psalms 107-150) range from the time of the prophets in the eighth century BC through to the rebuilding of the Temple and the re-establishing of the people of God as a worshipping community in Jerusalem once more.

It is better to understand the Psalter not primarily in terms of an individual author, but as produced by a community of faith who over the centuries composed, collected and passed on their prayers and songs as a witness to their experience as the people of God. While there were obviously 'authors' of these poems, the significance of the Psalms lies not in who wrote them, but in what they communicate about a response to God in a relationship with him and the world around us. From the Psalms we can learn that faith is a living relationship with God, expressed through our relationship with the world and each other.

READING PLAN

A plan for reading the Psalter through in thirty days, following the traditional pattern of reading Psalms each morning and evening, though the readings for each day could be read in one sitting.

	MORNING	EVENING
Day 1	Psalms 1–5	Psalms 6–8
Day 2	Psalms 9–11	Psalms 12–14
Day 3	Psalms 15–17	Psalm 18
Day 4	Psalms 19–21	Psalms 22–23
Day 5	Psalms 24–26	Psalms 27–29
Day 6	Psalms 30–31	Psalms 32–34
Day 7	Psalms 35–36	Psalm 37
Day 8	Psalms 38–40	Psalms 41–43
Day 9	Psalms 44–46	Psalms 47–49
Day 10	Psalms 50–52	Psalms 53–55
Day 11	Psalms 56–58	Psalms 59–61
Day 12	Psalms 62–64	Psalms 65–67
Day 13	Psalm 68	Psalms 69–70
Day 14	Psalms 71–72	Psalms 73–74
Day 15	Psalms 75–77	Psalm 78
Day 16	Psalms 79–81	Psalms 82–85
Day 17	Psalms 86–88	Psalm 89
Day 18	Psalms 90–92	Psalms 93–94
Day 19	Psalms 95–97	Psalms 98–101
Day 20	Psalms 102–103	Psalm 104
Day 21	Psalm 105	Psalm 106

PSALMS OF PRAISE:
    God of all creation: 8, 19, 29, 65 104, 114
    God's faithfulness and care: 33, 36, 103, 107, 111,
        117, 136, 139, 145, 146
    The majesty of God: 68, 76, 113,147,148, 149,
        150
    Historic acts of God: 78, 80, 81, 105, 106, 135
    God, King and Judge: 47, 50, 82, 93, 96, 97, 98, 99
    For guidance and loving kindness: 9, 18, 30, 34,
        67, 89, 92, 116, 118, 124,126, 136, 138

GUIDANCE FOR LIVING: 1, 15, 19, 26, 37, 49,
73, 112, 119, 127, 128, 133, 141

WHEN FAITH IS CHALLENGED: 6, 10, 22, 38,
39, 53,55, 79, 88, 120, 123, 130, 137, 140,142,
143

HOPE IN TROUBLE: 16, 23, 27, 32, 40, 42, 43, 46, 52, 56, 57, 61,62, 63, 73, 75, 91,112, 115, 121, 131

FROM COMPLAINT TO AWARENESS AND PRAISE:
Individual: 3, 4, 5, 11, 13, 17, 25, 28, 31, 41, 51 69, 70, 71, 77, 86, 102.
Nation: 12, 14, 44, 45, 60, 64, 74, 85, 90

HALLEL PSALMS: 113–118

PILGRIM PSALMS: 46, 48, 84, 87
The Songs of Ascents 120–134

IMPRECATORY PSALMS (contain curses or prayers for the punishment of the Psalmist's enemies): 7, 35, 55, 58, 59, 69, 79, 94, 108, 109, 137, 139, 143

PSALMS

PSALM 1

THE TWO PATHS

1 How blessed is anyone who rejects the advice of the
    wicked
  and does not take a stand in the path that sinners tread,
  nor a seat in company with cynics,
2 but who delights in the law of Yahweh
  and murmurs his law day and night.

3 Such a one is like a tree planted near streams;
  it bears fruit in season
  and its leaves never wither,
  and every project succeeds.
4 How different the wicked, how different!

  Just like chaff blown around by the wind
5 the wicked will not stand firm at the Judgement
  nor sinners in the gathering of the upright.
6 For Yahweh watches over the path of the upright,
  but the path of the wicked is doomed.

PSALM 2

THE MESSIANIC DRAMA

1 Why this uproar among the nations,
   this impotent muttering of the peoples?
2 Kings of the earth take up position,
   princes plot together
   against Yahweh and his anointed,
3 'Now let us break their fetters!
   Now let us throw off their bonds!'

4 He who is enthroned in the heavens laughs,
   Yahweh makes a mockery of them,
5 then in his anger rebukes them,
   in his rage he strikes them with terror.
6 'I myself have anointed my king
   on Zion my holy mountain.'

7 I will proclaim the decree of Yahweh:
   He said to me, 'You are my son,
   today have I fathered you.
8 Ask of me, and I shall give you the nations as your
      birthright,
   the whole wide world as your possession.
9 With an iron sceptre you will break them,
   shatter them like so many pots.'

10 So now, you kings, come to your senses,

you earthly rulers, learn your lesson!
¹¹ In fear be submissive to Yahweh;
¹² with trembling kiss his feet,
    lest he be angry and your way come to nothing,
    for his fury flares up in a moment.

How blessed are all who take refuge in him!

PSALM 3

MORNING PRAYER OF THE UPRIGHT IN PERSECUTION

Psalm   Of David   When he was fleeing from his son Absalom

¹ Yahweh, how countless are my enemies,
    how countless those who rise up against me,
² how countless those who say of me,
' No salvation for him from his God!'   *Pause*

³ But you, Yahweh, the shield at my side,
    my glory, you hold my head high.
⁴ I cry out to Yahweh;
    he answers from his holy mountain.   *Pause*

⁵ As for me, if I lie down and sleep,
    I shall awake, for Yahweh sustains me.
⁶ I have no fear of people in their thousands upon
        thousands,

who range themselves against me wherever I turn.

7 Arise, Yahweh, rescue me, my God!
You strike all my foes across the face,
you break the teeth of the wicked.
8 In Yahweh is salvation,
on your people, your blessing!   *Pause*

PSALM 4

EVENING PRAYER

For the choirmaster   For strings   Psalm   Of David

1 When I call, answer me, God, upholder of my right.
In my distress you have set me at large;
take pity on me and hear my prayer!

2 Children of men, how long will you be heavy of heart,
why love what is vain and chase after illusions?   *Pause*

3 Realise that Yahweh performs wonders for his faithful,
Yahweh listens when I call to him.

4 Be careful not to sin,
speak in your hearts, and on your beds keep silence.

                                                  Pause

5 Loyally offer sacrifices, and trust in Yahweh.

⁶ Many keep saying, 'Who will put happiness before
    our eyes?'
Let the light of your face shine on us.

Yahweh, ⁷to my heart you are a richer joy
than all their corn and new wine.

⁸ In peace I lie down and at once fall asleep,
    for it is you and none other, Yahweh, who make me
        rest secure.

PSALM 5

MORNING PRAYER

For the choirmaster   For flutes   Psalm Of David

¹ Give ear to my words, Yahweh,
    spare a thought for my sighing.
² Listen to my cry for help,
    my King and my God!

To you I pray, ³Yahweh.
    At daybreak you hear my voice;
at daybreak I lay my case before you
    and fix my eyes on you.

⁴ You are not a God who takes pleasure in evil,
    no sinner can be your guest.

⁵ Boasters cannot stand their ground
  under your gaze.

You hate evil-doers,
  ⁶ liars you destroy;
the violent and deceitful
  Yahweh detests.

⁷ But, so great is your faithful love,
  I may come into your house,
and before your holy temple
  bow down in reverence of you.

⁸ In your saving justice, Yahweh, lead me,
  because of those who lie in wait for me;
make your way plain before me.

⁹ Not a word from their lips can be trusted,
  through and through they are destruction,
their throats are wide-open graves,
  their tongues seductive.

¹⁰ Lay the guilt on them, God,
  make their intrigues their own downfall;
for their countless offences, thrust them from you,
  since they have rebelled against you.

¹¹ But joy for all who take refuge in you,

endless songs of gladness!
You shelter them, they rejoice in you,
those who love your name.

¹² It is you who bless the upright, Yahweh,
you surround them with favour as with a shield.

PSALM 6

SUPPLICATION IN TIME OF TRIAL

*For the choirmaster   For strings   For the octachord
Psalm   Of David*

¹ Yahweh, let your rebuke to me not be in anger,
your punishment not in the heat of wrath.
² Have pity on me, Yahweh, for I am fading away.
Heal me, Yahweh, my bones are shaken,
³ my spirit is shaken to its very depths.
But you, Yahweh … how long?

⁴ Yahweh, relent and save my life
rescue me because of your faithful love,
⁵ for in death there is no remembrance of you;
who could sing your praises in Sheol?

⁶ I am worn out with groaning,
every night I drench my pillow
and soak my bed with tears.

⁷ My eyes waste away with vexation.
    Arrogance from all my foes!
⁸ Away from me, all evil-doers!

    For Yahweh has heard the sound of my weeping,
⁹ Yahweh has heard my pleading.
    Yahweh will accept my prayer.
¹⁰ Let all my enemies be put to confusion, shaken to their
      depths,
    let them retreat in sudden confusion.

PSALM 7

PRAYER OF THE UPRIGHT IN PERSECUTION

Lament   Of David   Which he sang to Yahweh about Cush the Benjaminite

¹ Yahweh my God, I take refuge in you,
    save me from all my pursuers and rescue me,
² or he will savage me like a lion,
    carry me off with no one to rescue me.

³ Yahweh my God, if I have done this:
    if injustice has stained my hands,
⁴ if I have repaid my ally with treachery
    or spared one who attacked me unprovoked,
⁵ may an enemy hunt me down and catch me,

may he trample my life into the ground
and crush my vital parts into the dust.   *Pause*

6 Arise, Yahweh, in your anger,
   rise up against the arrogance of my foes.
        Awake, my God,
        you demand judgement.
7 Let the assembly of nations gather round you;
        return above it on high!
8 (Yahweh judges the nations.)

   Judge me, Yahweh, as my uprightness
        and my integrity deserve.
9 Put an end to the malice of the wicked,
        make the upright stand firm,
   you who discern hearts and minds,
        God the upright.

10 God is a shield that protects me,
        saving the honest of heart.
11 God is an upright judge,
        slow to anger,
        but a God at all times threatening
12 for those who will not repent.

   Let the enemy whet his sword,
   draw his bow and make ready;
13 but he is making ready instruments of death for himself

and tipping his arrows with fire;
¹⁴ look at him: pregnant with malice,
   conceiving spite, he gives birth to treachery.

¹⁵ He digs a trap, scoops it out,
   but he falls into the snare he made himself.
¹⁶ His spite recoils on his own head,
   his brutality falls back on his own skull.

¹⁷ I thank Yahweh for his saving justice.
   I sing to the name of the Most High.

PSALM 8

THE POWER OF GOD'S NAME

For the choirmaster   On the ... of Gatha   Psalm Of David

¹ Yahweh our Lord,
   how majestic is your name throughout the world!

Whoever keeps singing of your majesty higher than
      the heavens,
² even through the mouths of children, or of babes in arms,
   you make him a fortress, firm against your foes,
   to subdue the enemy and the rebel.

³ I look up at your heavens, shaped by your fingers,
   at the moon and the stars you set firm—

⁴ what are human beings that you spare a thought for
   them,
   or the child of Adam that you care for him?

⁵ Yet you have made him little less than a god,
   you have crowned him with glory and beauty,
⁶ made him lord of the works of your hands,
   put all things under his feet,

⁷ sheep and cattle, all of them,
   and even the wild beasts,
⁸ birds in the sky, fish in the sea,
   when he makes his way across the ocean.

⁹ Yahweh our Lord,
   how majestic your name throughout the world!

PSALMS 9-10

GOD STRIKES THE WICKED AND SAVES THE HUMBLE

For the choirmaster   On oboe and harp   Psalm Of David

Aleph   ¹ I thank you, Yahweh, with my whole heart,
           I recount all your wonders,
         ² I rejoice and delight in you,
           I sing to your name, Most High.

Bet
³ My enemies are in retreat,
    they stumble and perish at your presence,
⁴ for you have given fair judgement in my
      favour,
    seated on your throne as upright judge.

Gimel
⁵ You have rebuked the nations, destroyed the
      wicked,
    blotted out their name for ever and ever;
⁶ the enemy is wiped out—mere ruins for ever—
    you have annihilated their cities, their memory
      has perished.

He
See, ⁷Yahweh is enthroned for ever,
    keeping his throne firm for judgement;
⁸ he will himself judge the world in
      uprightness,
    will give a true verdict on the nations.

Waw
⁹ May Yahweh be a stronghold for the oppressed,
    a stronghold in times of trouble!
¹⁰ Those who revere your name can rely on you,
    you never desert those who seek you, Yahweh.

Zain
¹¹ Sing to Yahweh who dwells in Zion,
    tell the nations his mighty deeds,
¹² for the avenger of blood does not forget them,
    he does not ignore the cry of the afflicted.

Het 13 Have pity on me, Yahweh, see my affliction,
       pull me back from the gates of death,
     14 that I may recount all your praises at the gates
          of the daughter of Zion
       and rejoice in your salvation.

Tet 15 The nations have fallen into the trap they made,
       their feet caught in the snare they laid.
     16 Yahweh has made himself known, given
          judgement,
       he has ensnared the wicked in the work of
          their own hands.   *Muted music Pause*

Yod 17 May the wicked turn away to Sheol,
       all the nations forgetful of God.
Kaph 18 For the needy is not forgotten for ever,
       not for ever does the hope of the poor come
          to nothing.

     19 Arise, Yahweh; human strength shall not prevail.
       The nations shall stand trial before you.
     20 Strike them with terror, Yahweh;
       the nations shall know that they are no
          more than human!   *Pause*

10

Lamed	¹ Why, Yahweh, do you keep so distant, stay hidden in times of trouble?
	² In his pride the wicked hunts down the weak, who is caught in the schemes he devises.
(Mem)	³ The wicked is proud of his inmost desires, by his blasphemies the grasping spurns Yahweh,
(Nun)	⁴ the wicked in his arrogance does not look very far; 'There is no God,' is his only thought.

⁵ In all circumstances his step is assured;
your judgements are above his head.
His rivals? He scoffs at them all.

⁶ He says in his heart, 'I shall never be shaken,'
free of trouble himself, ⁷he wishes it on others.

(Samek)
Pe

His speech is full of lies and browbeating,
under his tongue lurk spite and wickedness.
⁸ In the undergrowth he lies in ambush,
in his hiding-place he murders the innocent.

Ain

He watches intently for the downtrodden,
⁹ lurking unseen like a lion in his lair,
lurking to pounce on the poor;
he pounces on him and drags him off in his net.

(Zade) ¹⁰ He keeps watch, crouching down low,
the poor wretch falls into his clutches;
¹¹ he says in his heart, 'God forgets,
he has turned away his face to avoid seeing the
end.'

Qoph ¹² Rise, Yahweh! God, raise your hand,
do not forget the afflicted!
¹³ Why should the wicked spurn God,
assuring himself you will never follow it up?

Resh ¹⁴ You have seen for yourself the trouble and
vexation,
you watch so as to take it in hand.
The oppressed relies on you;
you are the only recourse of the orphan.

Shin ¹⁵ Break the arm of the wicked and evil,
seek out wickedness till there is none left to
be found.
¹⁶ Yahweh is king for ever and ever,
the heathen has vanished from his country.

Taw ¹⁷ Yahweh, you listen to the laments of the poor,
you give them courage, you grant them a
hearing,
¹⁸ to give judgement for the orphaned and
exploited,

so that earthborn humans may strike terror no
more.

PSALM 11

THE CONFIDENCE OF THE UPRIGHT

For the choirmaster   Of David

¹ In Yahweh I have found refuge.
  How can you say to me,
' Bird, flee to your mountain?

² 'For look, the wicked are drawing their bows,
  fitting their arrows to the string
  to shoot honest men from the shadows.
³ If the foundations fall to ruin, what can the upright do?'

⁴ Yahweh in his holy temple!
  Yahweh, his throne is in heaven;
  his eyes watch over the world,
  his gaze scrutinises the children of Adam.

⁵ Yahweh examines the upright and the wicked,
  the lover of violence he detests.
⁶ He will rain down red–hot coals,
  fire and sulphur on the wicked,
  a scorching wind will be their lot.

7 For Yahweh is upright and loves uprightness,
   the honest will ever see his face.

PSALM 12

AGAINST A TREACHEROUS WORLD

For the choirmaster   On the octachord   Psalm Of David

1 Help, Yahweh! No one loyal is left,
   the faithful have vanished from among the children
      of Adam.
2 Friend tells lies to friend,
   and, smooth-tongued, speaks from an insincere heart.

3 May Yahweh cut away every smooth lip,
   every boastful tongue,
4 those who say, 'In our tongue lies our strength,
   our lips are our allies; who can master us?'
5 'For the poor who are plundered, the needy who groan,
   now will I act,' says Yahweh,
   'I will grant salvation to those who sigh for it.'

6 Yahweh's promises are promises unalloyed,
   natural silver which comes from the earth seven
      times refined.

7 You, Yahweh, will watch over them,
   you will protect them from that brood for ever.

⁸ The wicked will scatter in every direction,
  as the height of depravity among the children of Adam.

PSALM 13

A CONFIDENT APPEAL

For the choirmaster   Psalm   Of David

¹ How long, Yahweh, will you forget me? For ever?
  How long will you turn away your face from me?
² How long must I nurse rebellion in my soul,
  sorrow in my heart day and night?
  How long is the enemy to domineer over me?
³ Look down, answer me, Yahweh my God!
  Give light to my eyes or I shall fall into the sleep of
      death.

⁴ Or my foe will boast, 'I have overpowered him,'
  and my enemy have the joy of seeing me stumble.
⁵ As for me, I trust in your faithful love, Yahweh.
  Let my heart delight in your saving help,
  let me sing to Yahweh for his generosity to me,
  let me sing to the name of Yahweh the Most High!

PSALM 14

THE FATE OF THE GODLESS

For the choirmaster   Of David

1 The fool has said in his heart,
       'There is no God.'
    Their deeds are corrupt and vile,
       not one of them does right.

2 Yahweh looks down from heaven
       at the children of Adam.
    To see if a single one is wise,
       a single one seeks God.
3 All have turned away,
       all alike turned sour,
    not one of them does right,
       not a single one.

4 Are they not aware, all these evil-doers?
       They are devouring my people,
       this is the bread they eat,
       and they never call to Yahweh.

5 They will be gripped with fear,
       where there is no need for fear,
    for God takes the side of the upright;
6 you may mock the plans of the poor,

but Yahweh is their refuge.

7 Who will bring from Zion salvation for Israel?
   When Yahweh brings his people home,
   what joy for Jacob, what happiness for Israel!

PSALM 15

THE GUEST OF YAHWEH

Psalm   Of David

1 Yahweh, who can find a home in your tent,
   who can dwell on your holy mountain?
2 Whoever lives blamelessly,
   who acts uprightly,
   who speaks the truth from the heart,
3 who keeps the tongue under control,

   who does not wrong a comrade,
   who casts no discredit on a neighbour,
4 who looks with scorn on the vile,
   but honours those who fear Yahweh,

   who stands by an oath at any cost,
5 who asks no interest on loans,
   who takes no bribe to harm the innocent.
   No one who so acts can ever be shaken.

PSALM 16

YAHWEH MY HERITAGE

In a quiet voice   Of David

¹ Protect me, O God, in you is my refuge.

² To Yahweh I say, 'You are my Lord,
    my happiness is in none ³of the sacred spirits of the
        earth.'

They only take advantage of all who love them.
⁴ People flock to their teeming idols.
    Never shall I pour libations to them!
    Never take their names on my lips.
⁵ My birthright, my cup is Yahweh;
    you, you alone, hold my lot secure.
⁶ The measuring-line marks out for me a delightful place,
    my birthright is all I could wish.

⁷ I bless Yahweh who is my counsellor,
    even at night my heart instructs me.
⁸ I keep Yahweh before me always,
    for with him at my right hand, nothing can shake me.

⁹ So my heart rejoices, my soul delights,
    my body too will rest secure,
¹⁰ for you will not abandon me to Sheol,

you cannot allow your faithful servant to see the abyss.
¹¹ You will teach me the path of life,
unbounded joy in your presence,
at your right hand delight for ever.

PSALM 17

THE PLEA OF THE INNOCENT

Prayer   Of David

¹ Listen, Yahweh, to an upright cause,
pay attention to my cry,
lend an ear to my prayer,
my lips free from deceit.
² From your presence will issue my vindication,
your eyes fixed on what is right.

³ You probe my heart, examine me at night,
you test me by fire and find no evil.
I have not sinned with my mouth ⁴as most people do.

I have treasured the word from your lips,
⁵ my steps never stray from the paths you lay down,
from your tracks; so my feet never stumble.
⁶ I call upon you, God, for you answer me;
turn your ear to me, hear what I say.
⁷ Show the evidence of your faithful love,
saviour of those who hope in your strength against attack.

⁸ Guard me as the pupil of an eye,
    shelter me in the shadow of your wings
⁹ from the presence of the wicked who would maltreat
        me;
    deadly enemies are closing in on me.
¹⁰ Engrossed in themselves
    they are mouthing arrogant words.
¹¹ They are advancing against me, now they are closing in,
    watching for the chance to hurl me to the ground,
¹² like a lion preparing to pounce,
    like a young lion crouching in ambush.

¹³ Arise, Yahweh, confront him and bring him down,
    with your sword save my life from the wicked,
¹⁴ Yahweh, from mortals, by your hand,
    from mortals whose part in life is in this world.

    You fill their bellies from your store,
    their children will have all they desire,
    and leave their surplus to their children.
¹⁵ But I in my uprightness will see your face,
    and when I awake I shall be filled with the vision of
        you.

PSALM 18

A KING'S THANKSGIVING

For the choirmaster Of David, the servant of Yahweh, who addressed the words of this song to Yahweh when Yahweh had delivered him from all his enemies and from the clutches of Saul. He said:

1 I love you, Yahweh, my strength
   (my Saviour, you have saved me from violence).

2 Yahweh is my rock and my fortress,
   my deliverer is my God.
   I take refuge in him, my rock,
   my shield, my saving strength,
   my stronghold, my place of refuge.

3 I call to Yahweh who is worthy of praise,
   and I am saved from my foes.

4 With Death's breakers closing in on me,
   Belial's torrents ready to swallow me,
5 Sheol's snares every side of me,
   Death's traps lying ahead of me,

6 I called to Yahweh in my anguish,
   I cried for help to my God;
   from his Temple he heard my voice,
   my cry came to his ears.

⁷ Then the earth quaked and rocked,
the mountains' foundations shuddered,
they quaked at his blazing anger.
⁸ Smoke rose from his nostrils,
from his mouth devouring fire
(coals were kindled at it).

⁹ He parted the heavens and came down,
a storm-cloud underneath his feet;
¹⁰ riding one of the winged creatures, he flew,
soaring on the wings of the wind.

¹¹ His covering he made the darkness,
his pavilion dark waters and dense cloud.
¹² A brightness lit up before him,
hail and blazing fire.

¹³ Yahweh thundered from the heavens,
the Most High made his voice heard.
¹⁴ He shot his arrows and scattered them,
he hurled his lightning and routed them.

¹⁵ The very springs of ocean were exposed,
the world's foundations were laid bare,
at your roaring, Yahweh,
at the blast of breath from your nostrils!

¹⁶ He reached down from on high, snatched me up,

pulled me from the watery depths,
¹⁷ rescued me from my mighty foe,
from my enemies who were stronger than I.

¹⁸ They assailed me on my day of disaster
but Yahweh was there to support me;
¹⁹ he freed me, set me at large,
he rescued me because he loves me.

²⁰ Yahweh rewards me for my uprightness,
as my hands are pure, so he repays me,
²¹ since I have kept the ways of Yahweh,
and not fallen away from my God.
²² His judgements are all before me,
his statutes I have not put away from me.
²³ I am blameless before him,
I keep myself clear of evil.

²⁴ So Yahweh repaid me for acting uprightly
because he could see I was pure.
²⁵ You are faithful to the faithful,
blameless with the blameless,

²⁶ sincere to the sincere,
but cunning to the crafty,
²⁷ you save a people that is humble
and humiliate those with haughty looks.

²⁸ Yahweh, you yourself are my lamp,
   my God lights up my darkness;
²⁹ with you I storm the rampart,
   with my God I can scale any wall.

³⁰ This God, his way is blameless;
   the word of Yahweh is refined in the furnace,
   for he alone is the shield
   of all who take refuge in him.

³¹ For who is God but Yahweh,
   who is a rock but our God?
³² This God who girds me with strength,
who makes my way free from blame,

³³ who makes me as swift as a deer
   and sets me firmly on the heights,
³⁴ who trains my hands for battle,
   my arms to bend a bow of bronze.

³⁵ You give me your invincible shield
   (your right hand upholds me)
   you never cease to listen to me,
³⁶ you give me the strides of a giant,
   give me ankles that never weaken.

³⁷ I pursue my enemies and overtake them,
   not turning back till they are annihilated;

³⁸ I strike them down and they cannot rise,
    they fall, they are under my feet.

³⁹ You have girded me with strength for the fight,
    bent down my assailants beneath me,
⁴⁰ made my enemies retreat before me;
    and those who hate me I destroy.

⁴¹ They cry out, there is no one to save;
    to Yahweh, but no answer comes.
⁴² I crumble them like dust before the wind,
    trample them like the mud of the streets.

⁴³ You free me from the quarrels of my people,
    you place me at the head of the nations,
    a people I did not know are now my servants;

⁴⁴ foreigners come wooing my favour,
    no sooner do they hear than they obey me;
⁴⁵ foreigners grow faint of heart,
    they come trembling out of their fastnesses.

⁴⁶ Life to Yahweh! Blessed be my rock!
    Exalted be the God of my salvation,
⁴⁷ the God who gives me vengeance,
    and subjects whole peoples to me,

⁴⁸ who rescues me from my raging enemies.

You lift me high above those who attack me,
  you deliver me from the man of violence.

⁴⁹ For this I will praise you, Yahweh, among the
      nations,
  and sing praise to your name.

⁵⁰ He saves his king time after time,
  displays his faithful love for his anointed,
  for David and his heirs for ever.

PSALM 19

YAHWEH, SUN OF SAVING JUSTICE

For the choirmaster   Psalm   Of David

¹ The heavens declare the glory of God,
  the vault of heaven proclaims his handiwork,
² day discourses of it to day,
  night to night hands on the knowledge.

³ No utterance at all, no speech,
  not a sound to be heard,
⁴ but from the entire earth the design stands out,
  this message reaches the whole world.

  High above, he pitched a tent for the sun,
⁵ who comes forth from his pavilion like a bridegroom,

delights like a champion in the course to be run.

6 Rising on the one horizon
  he runs his circuit to the other,
  and nothing can escape his heat.

7 The Law of Yahweh is perfect,
      refreshment to the soul;
  the decree of Yahweh is trustworthy,
      wisdom for the simple.

8 The precepts of Yahweh are honest,
      joy for the heart;
  the commandment of Yahweh is pure,
      light for the eyes.

9 The fear of Yahweh is pure,
      lasting for ever;
  the judgements of Yahweh are true,
      upright, every one,

10 more desirable than gold,
      even than the finest gold;
  his words are sweeter than honey,
      that drips from the comb.

11 Thus your servant is formed by them;
      observing them brings great reward.

¹² But who can detect his own failings?
    Wash away my hidden faults.

¹³ And from pride preserve your servant,
        never let it be my master.
    So shall I be above reproach,
        free from grave sin.

¹⁴ May the words of my mouth always find favour,
        and the whispering of my heart,
    in your presence, Yahweh,
        my rock, my redeemer.

PSALM 20

PRAYER FOR THE KING

For the choirmaster   Psalm   Of David

¹ May Yahweh answer you in time of trouble,
    may the name of the God of Jacob protect you!
² May he send you help from the sanctuary,
    give you support from Zion!

³ May he remember all your sacrifices
    and delight in your burnt offerings!   *Pause*
⁴ May he grant you your heart's desire
    and crown all your plans with success!

5 So that with joy we can hail your victory
and draw up our ranks in the name of our God.

May Yahweh grant all your petitions.

6 Now I know that Yahweh
gives victory to his anointed.
He will respond from his holy heavens
with great deeds of victory from his right hand.

7 Some call on chariots, some on horses,
but we on the name of Yahweh our God.
8 They will crumple and fall,
while we stand upright and firm.

9 Yahweh, save the king,
answer us when we call.

PSALM 21

FOR A CORONATION CEREMONY

For the choirmaster   Psalm   Of David

1 Yahweh, the king rejoices in your power;
How your saving help fills him with joy!
2 You have granted him his heart's desire,
not denied him the prayer of his lips.   *Pause*

3 For you come to meet him with blessings of prosperity,
   put a crown of pure gold on his head.
4 He has asked for life, you have given it him,
   length of days for ever and ever.

5 Great his glory through your saving help;
   you invest him with splendour and majesty.
6 You confer on him everlasting blessings,
   you gladden him with the joy of your presence.
7 For the king puts his trust in Yahweh;
   the faithful love of the Most High will keep him from
      falling.
8 Your hand will reach all your enemies,
   your right hand all who hate you.
9 You will hurl them into a blazing furnace
   on the day when you appear;
   Yahweh will engulf them in his anger,
   and fire will devour them.
10 You will purge the earth of their descendants,
   the human race of their posterity.

11 They have devised evil against you
   but, plot as they may, they will not succeed,
12 since you will make them turn tail,
   by shooting your arrows in their faces.

13 Rise, Yahweh, in your power!
   We will sing and make music in honour of your strength.

PSALM 22

THE SUFFERINGS AND HOPES OF THE UPRIGHT

For the choirmaster   To 'the Doe of the Dawn'   Psalm Of David

¹ My God, my God, why have you forsaken me?
   The words of my groaning do nothing to save me.

² My God, I call by day but you do not answer,
   at night, but I find no respite.

³ Yet you, the Holy One,
   who make your home in the praises of Israel,

⁴ in you our ancestors put their trust,
   they trusted and you set them free.

⁵ To you they called for help and were delivered;
   in you they trusted and were not put to shame.

⁶ But I am a worm, less than human,
   scorn of mankind, contempt of the people;

⁷ all who see me jeer at me,
   they sneer and wag their heads,

⁸ 'He trusted himself to Yahweh, let Yahweh set him free!
   Let him deliver him, as he took such delight in him.'

⁹ It was you who drew me from the womb
   and soothed me on my mother's breast.

¹⁰ On you was I cast from my birth,
   from the womb I have belonged to you.

¹¹ Do not hold aloof, for trouble is upon me,
and no one to help me!

¹² Many bulls are encircling me,
wild bulls of Bashan closing in on me.
¹³ Lions ravening and roaring
open their jaws at me.

¹⁴ My strength is trickling away,
my bones are all disjointed,
my heart has turned to wax,
melting inside me.
¹⁵ My mouth is dry as earthenware,
my tongue sticks to my jaw.
You lay me down in the dust of death.

¹⁶ A pack of dogs surrounds me,
a gang of villains closing in on me
as if to hack off my hands and my feet.
¹⁷ I can count every one of my bones,
while they look on and gloat;
¹⁸ they divide my garments among them
and cast lots for my clothing.

¹⁹ Yahweh, do not hold aloof!
My strength, come quickly to my help,
²⁰ rescue my soul from the sword,
the one life I have from the grasp of the dog!

²¹ Save me from the lion's mouth,
   my poor life from the wild bulls' horns!

²² I shall proclaim your name to my brothers,
   praise you in full assembly:
²³ 'You who fear Yahweh, praise him!
   All the race of Jacob, honour him!
   Revere him, all the race of Israel!'
²⁴ For he has not despised
   nor disregarded the poverty of the poor,
   has not turned away his face,
   but has listened to the cry for help.

²⁵ Of you is my praise in the thronged assembly,
   I will perform my vows before all who fear him.
²⁶ The poor will eat and be filled,
   those who seek Yahweh will praise him,
   'May your heart live for ever.'

²⁷ The whole wide world will remember and return to
      Yahweh,
   all the families of nations bow down before him.
²⁸ For to Yahweh, ruler of the nations, belongs kingly
      power!
²⁹ All who prosper on earth will bow before him,
   all who go down to the dust will do reverence before him.
   And those who are dead, ³⁰their descendants will
      serve him,

will proclaim his name to generations [31]still to come;
and these will tell of his saving justice to a people yet
    unborn:
he has fulfilled it.

PSALM 23

THE GOOD SHEPHERD

Psalm   Of David

[1] Yahweh is my shepherd, I lack nothing.
[2] In grassy meadows he lets me lie.

By tranquil streams he leads me
    [3] to restore my spirit.
He guides me in paths of saving justice
    as befits his name.

[4] Even were I to walk in a ravine as dark as death
I should fear no danger, for you are at my side.
Your staff and your crook are there to soothe me.

[5] You prepare a table for me
    under the eyes of my enemies;
you anoint my head with oil;
    my cup brims over.

⁶ Kindness and faithful love pursue me
    every day of my life.
I make my home in the house of Yahweh
    for all time to come.

PSALM 24

FOR A SOLEMN ENTRY INTO THE SANCTUARY

Psalm   Of David

¹ To Yahweh belong the earth and all it contains,
    the world and all who live there;
² it is he who laid its foundations on the seas,
    on the flowing waters fixed it firm.

³ Who shall go up to the mountain of Yahweh?
    Who shall take a stand in his holy place?

⁴ The clean of hands and pure of heart,
    whose heart is not set on vanities,
    who does not swear an oath in order to deceive.

⁵ Such a one will receive blessing from Yahweh,
    saving justice from the God of his salvation.
⁶ Such is the people that seeks him,
    that seeks your presence, God of Jacob.   *Pause*

7   Gates, lift high your heads,
    raise high the ancient gateways,
    and the king of glory shall enter!

8   Who is he, this king of glory?
    It is Yahweh, strong and valiant,
    Yahweh valiant in battle.

9   Gates, lift high your heads,
    raise high the ancient gateways,
    and the king of glory shall enter!

10 Who is he, this king of glory?
    Yahweh Sabaoth,
    he is the king of glory.   *Pause*

PSALM 25

PRAYER IN DANGER

Of David

Aleph   1   ADORATION I offer, Yahweh,
          2   to you, my God.

Bet   BUT in my trust in you do not put me to
                   shame,
               let not my enemies gloat over me.

Gimel   ³ CALLING to you, none shall ever be put to
shame,
but shame is theirs who groundlessly break faith.

Dalet   ⁴ DIRECT me in your ways, Yahweh,
and teach me your paths.

He   ⁵ ENCOURAGE me to walk in your truth
and teach me
since you are the God who saves me.

(Waw)   FOR my hope is in you all day long—
such is your generosity, Yahweh.

Zain   ⁶ GOODNESS and faithful love have been
yours for ever,
Yahweh, do not forget them.

Het   ⁷ HOLD not my youthful sins against me,
but remember me as your faithful love dictates.

Tet   ⁸ INTEGRITY and generosity are marks of
Yahweh
for he brings sinners back to the path.

Yod   ⁹ JUDICIOUSLY he guides the humble,
instructing the poor in his way.

Kaph   ¹⁰ KINDNESS unfailing and constancy mark all
Yahweh's paths,

> for those who keep his covenant and his
> decrees.

Lamed 11 LET my sin, great though it is, be forgiven,
> Yahweh, for the sake of your name.

Mem 12 MEN who respect Yahweh, what of them?
> He teaches them the way they must choose.

Nun 13 NEIGHBOURS to happiness will they live,
> and their children inherit the land.

Samek 14 ONLY those who fear Yahweh have his secret
> and his covenant, for their understanding.

Ain 15 PERMANENTLY my eyes are on Yahweh,
> for he will free my feet from the snare.

Pe 16 QUICK, turn to me, pity me,
> alone and wretched as I am!

Zade 17 RELIEVE the distress of my heart,
> bring me out of my constraint.

(Qoph) 18 SPARE a glance for my misery and pain,
> take all my sins away.

Resh 19 TAKE note how countless are my enemies,
> how violent their hatred for me.

Shin 20 UNLESS you guard me and rescue me
> I shall be put to shame, for you are my refuge.

Taw 21 VIRTUE and integrity be my protection,
> for my hope, Yahweh, is in you.

²² Ransom Israel, O God,
    from all its troubles.

PSALM 26

PRAYER OF THE BLAMELESS

Of David

¹ Yahweh, be my judge!
  I go on my way in innocence,
  my trust in Yahweh never wavers.

² Probe me, Yahweh, examine me,
  Test my heart and my mind in the fire.
³ For your faithful love is before my eyes,
  and I live my life by your truth.

⁴ No sitting with wastrels for me,
  no travelling with hypocrites;
⁵ I hate the company of sinners,
  I refuse to sit down with the wicked.

⁶ I will wash my hands in innocence
  and join the procession round your altar, Yahweh,
⁷ to make heard the sound of thanksgiving,
  to proclaim all your wonders.
⁸ Yahweh, I love the beauty of your house
  and the place where your glory dwells.

⁹ Do not couple me with sinners,
   nor my life with men of violence,
¹⁰ whose hands are stained with guilt,
   their right hands heavy with bribes.

¹¹ In innocence I will go on my way;
   ransom me, take pity on me.
¹² I take my stand on the right path;
   I will bless you, Yahweh, in the assemblies.

PSALM 27

IN GOD'S COMPANY THERE IS NO FEAR

Of David

¹ Yahweh is my light and my salvation,
      whom should I fear?
   Yahweh is the fortress of my life,
      whom should I dread?

² When the wicked advance against me
      to eat me up,
   they, my opponents, my enemies,
      are the ones who stumble and fall.

³ Though an army pitch camp against me,
      my heart will not fear,

though war break out against me,
my trust will never be shaken.

4 One thing I ask of Yahweh,
one thing I seek:
to dwell in Yahweh's house
all the days of my life,
to enjoy the sweetness of Yahweh,
to seek out his temple.

5 For he hides me away under his roof
on the day of evil,
he folds me in the recesses of his tent,
sets me high on a rock.
6 Now my head is held high
above the enemies who surround me;
in his tent I will offer
sacrifices of acclaim.

I will sing, I will make music for Yahweh.

7 Yahweh, hear my voice as I cry,
pity me, answer me!
8 Of you my heart has said,
'Seek his face!'
Your face, Yahweh, I seek;
9 do not turn away from me.

Do not thrust aside your servant in anger,
   without you I am helpless.
Never leave me, never forsake me,
   God, my Saviour.
10 Though my father and mother forsake me,
   Yahweh will gather me up.

11 Yahweh, teach me your way,
   lead me on the path of integrity
      because of my enemies;
12 do not abandon me to the will of my foes—
   false witnesses have risen against me,
      and are breathing out violence.

13 This I believe: I shall see the goodness of Yahweh,
   in the land of the living.
14 Put your hope in Yahweh, be strong, let your heart be
      bold,
   put your hope in Yahweh.

PSALM 28

PETITION AND THANKSGIVING

Of David

1 To you, Yahweh, I cry,
   my rock, do not be deaf to me!

If you stay silent
    I shall be like those who sink into oblivion.

2 Hear the sound of my prayer
    when I call upon you,
when I raise my hands, Yahweh,
    towards your Holy of Holies.

3 Do not drag me away with the wicked,
    with evil-doers,
who talk to their partners of peace
    with treachery in their hearts.

4 Repay them as their deeds deserve,
    as befits their treacherous actions;
as befits their handiwork repay them,
    let their deserts fall back on themselves.

5 They do not comprehend the deeds of Yahweh,
    the work of his hands.
May he pull them down and not rebuild them!

6 Blessed be Yahweh
for he hears the sound of my prayer.

7 Yahweh is my strength and my shield,
    in him my heart trusts.
I have been helped; my body has recovered its vigour,

with all my heart I thank him.

8 Yahweh is the strength of his people,
    a safe refuge for his anointed.
9 Save your people, bless your heritage,
    shepherd them and carry them for ever!

PSALM 29

HYMN TO THE LORD OF THE STORM

Psalm   Of David

1 Give Yahweh his due, sons of God,
    give Yahweh his due of glory and strength,
2 give Yahweh the glory due to his name,
    adore Yahweh in the splendour of holiness.

3 Yahweh's voice over the waters, the God of glory
        thunders;
    Yahweh over countless waters,
4 Yahweh's voice in power, Yahweh's voice in splendour;
5 Yahweh's voice shatters cedars,
    Yahweh shatters cedars of Lebanon,
6 he makes Lebanon skip like a calf,
    Sirion like a young wild ox.

7 Yahweh's voice carves out lightning-shafts,
8 Yahweh's voice convulses the desert,

Yahweh convulses the desert of Kadesh,
9 Yahweh's voice convulses terebinths,
strips forests bare.

In his palace all cry, 'Glory!'
10 Yahweh was enthroned for the flood,
Yahweh is enthroned as king for ever.
11 Yahweh will give strength to his people,
Yahweh blesses his people with peace.

PSALM 30

THANKSGIVING AFTER MORTAL DANGER

Psalm   Canticle for the Dedication of the House   Of David

1 I praise you to the heights, Yahweh, for you have raised
    me up,
   you have not let my foes make merry over me.
2 Yahweh, my God, I cried to you for help and you
    healed me.
3 Yahweh, you have lifted me out of Sheol,
   from among those who sink into oblivion you have
    given me life.

4 Make music for Yahweh, all you who are faithful to him,
   praise his unforgettable holiness.
5 His anger lasts but a moment, his favour through life;

In the evening come tears, but with dawn cries of joy.

6 Carefree, I used to think,
  'Nothing can ever shake me!'
7 Your favour, Yahweh, set me on impregnable heights,
  but you turned away your face and I was terrified.

8 To you, Yahweh, I call,
  to my God I cry for mercy.
9 What point is there in my death, my going down to
    the abyss?
  Can the dust praise you or proclaim your faithfulness?

10 Listen, Yahweh, take pity on me,
  Yahweh, be my help!
11 You have turned my mourning into dancing,
  you have stripped off my sackcloth and clothed me
    with joy.
12 So my heart will sing to you unceasingly,
  Yahweh, my God, I shall praise you for ever.

PSALM 31

PRAYER IN TIME OF ORDEAL

For the choirmaster Psalm Of David

1 In you, Yahweh, I have taken refuge,
  let me never be put to shame,

in your saving justice deliver me, rescue me,
² turn your ear to me, make haste.

Be for me a rock-fastness,
a fortified citadel to save me.
³ You are my rock, my rampart;
true to your name, lead me and guide me!

⁴ Draw me out of the net they have spread for me,
for you are my refuge;
⁵ to your hands I commit my spirit,
by you have I been redeemed.

God of truth, ⁶you hate
those who serve useless idols;
but my trust is in Yahweh:
⁷ I will delight and rejoice in your faithful love!

You, who have seen my misery,
and witnessed the miseries of my soul,
⁸ have not handed me over to the enemy,
but have given me freedom to roam at large.

⁹ Take pity on me, Yahweh,
for I am in trouble.
Vexation is gnawing away my eyes,
my soul deep within me.

¹⁰ For my life is worn out with sorrow,
and my years with sighs.
My strength gives way under my misery,
and my bones are all wasted away.

¹¹ The sheer number of my enemies
makes me contemptible,
loathsome to my neighbours,
and my friends shrink from me in horror.

When people see me in the street
they take to their heels.
¹² I have no more place in their hearts than a corpse,
or something lost.

¹³ All I hear is slander
—terror wherever I turn—
as they plot together against me,
scheming to take my life.

¹⁴ But my trust is in you, Yahweh;
I say, 'You are my God,'
¹⁵ every moment of my life is in your hands, rescue me
from the clutches of my foes who pursue me;
¹⁶ let your face shine on your servant,
save me in your faithful love.

¹⁷ I call on you, Yahweh, so let disgrace fall not on me,

but on the wicked.
Let them go down to Sheol in silence,
[18] muzzles on their lying mouths,
which speak arrogantly against the upright
in pride and contempt.

[19] Yahweh, what quantities of good things
you have in store for those who fear you,
and bestow on those who make you their refuge,
for all humanity to see.

[20] Safe in your presence you hide them,
far from human plotting,
shielding them in your tent,
far from contentious tongues.

[21] Blessed be Yahweh who works for me
miracles of his faithful love
(in a fortified city)!
[22] In a state of terror I cried,
'I have been cut off from your sight!'
Yet you heard my plea for help
when I cried out to you.

[23] Love Yahweh, all his faithful:
Yahweh protects his loyal servants,
but he repays the arrogant
with interest.

²⁴ Be brave, take heart,
all who put your hope in Yahweh.

PSALM 32 V 31

CANDID ADMISSION OF SIN

Of David   Poem

¹ How blessed are those whose offence is forgiven,
whose sin blotted out.
² How blessed are those to whom Yahweh imputes no
guilt,
whose spirit harbours no deceit.

³ I said not a word, but my bones wasted away
from groaning all the day;
⁴ day and night
your hand lay heavy upon me;
my heart grew parched as stubble
in summer drought.   *Pause*
⁵ I made my sin known to you,
did not conceal my guilt.
I said, 'I shall confess
my offence to Yahweh.'
And you, for your part, took away my guilt,
forgave my sin.   *Pause*

⁶ That is why each of your faithful ones prays to you

in time of distress.
Even if great floods overflow,
   they will never reach your faithful.
7 You are a refuge for me,
   you guard me in trouble,
with songs of deliverance you surround me.   *Pause*

8 I shall instruct you and teach you the way to go;
I shall not take my eyes off you.

9 Be not like a horse or a mule;
   that does not understand bridle or bit;
   if you advance to master them,
there is no means of bringing them near.

10 Countless troubles are in store for the wicked,
   but one who trusts in Yahweh is enfolded in his
      faithful love.

11 Rejoice in Yahweh,
   exult all you upright,
   shout for joy, you honest of heart.

PSALM 33

HYMN TO PROVIDENCE

¹ Shout for joy, you upright;
  praise comes well from the honest.
² Give thanks to Yahweh on the lyre,
  play for him on the ten-stringed lyre.
³ Sing to him a new song,
  make sweet music for your cry of victory.

⁴ The word of Yahweh is straightforward,
  all he does springs from his constancy.
⁵ He loves uprightness and justice;
  the faithful love of Yahweh fills the earth.

⁶ By the word of Yahweh the heavens were made,
  by the breath of his mouth all their array.
⁷ He collects the waters of the sea like a dam,
  he stores away the abyss in his treasure-house.

⁸ Let the whole earth fear Yahweh,
  let all who dwell in the world revere him;
⁹ for, the moment he spoke, it was so,
  no sooner had he commanded, than there it stood!
¹⁰ Yahweh thwarts the plans of nations,
  frustrates the counsels of peoples;
¹¹ but Yahweh's own plan stands firm for ever,

his heart's counsel from age to age.
¹² How blessed the nation whose God is Yahweh,
the people he has chosen as his heritage.

¹³ From heaven Yahweh looks down,
he sees all the children of Adam,
¹⁴ from the place where he sits he watches
all who dwell on the earth;
¹⁵ he alone moulds their hearts,
he understands all they do.

¹⁶ A large army will not keep a king safe,
nor his strength save a warrior's life;
¹⁷ it is delusion to rely on a horse for safety,
for all its power it cannot save.

¹⁸ But see how Yahweh watches over those who fear
him,
those who rely on his faithful love,
¹⁹ to rescue them from death
and keep them alive in famine.

²⁰ We are waiting for Yahweh;
he is our help and our shield,
²¹ for in him our heart rejoices,
in his holy name we trust.
²² Yahweh, let your faithful love rest on us,
as our hope has rested in you.

PSALM 34

IN PRAISE OF GOD'S JUSTICE

Of David, when he had feigned insanity before Abimelech, and Abimelech sent him away

Aleph	1	I will bless Yahweh at all times, his praise continually on my lips.
Bet	2	I will praise Yahweh from my heart; let the humble hear and rejoice.
Gimel	3	Proclaim with me the greatness of Yahweh, let us acclaim his name together.
Dalet	4	I seek Yahweh and he answers me, frees me from all my fears.
He	5	Fix your gaze on Yahweh and your face will grow bright, you will never hang your head in shame.
Zain	6	A pauper calls out and Yahweh hears, saves him from all his troubles.
Het	7	The angel of Yahweh encamps around those who fear him, and rescues them.
Tet	8	Taste and see that Yahweh is good. How blessed are those who take refuge in him.

Yod	9 Fear Yahweh, you his holy ones; those who fear him lack for nothing.
Kaph	10 Young lions may go needy and hungry, but those who seek Yahweh lack nothing good.
Lamed	11 Come, my children, listen to me, I will teach you the fear of Yahweh.
Mem	12 Who among you delights in life, longs for time to enjoy prosperity?
Nun	13 Guard your tongue from evil, your lips from any breath of deceit.
Samek	14 Turn away from evil and do good, seek peace and pursue it.
Ain	15 The eyes of Yahweh are on the upright, his ear turned to their cry.
Pe	16 But Yahweh's face is set against those who do evil, to cut off the memory of them from the earth.
Zade	17 They cry in anguish and Yahweh hears, and rescues them from all their troubles.
Qoph	18 Yahweh is near to the broken-hearted, he helps those whose spirit is crushed.
Resh	19 Though hardships without number beset the upright,

Yahweh brings rescue from them all.

Shin   20 Yahweh takes care of all their bones,
not one of them will be broken.

Taw   21 But to the wicked evil brings death,
those who hate the upright will pay the
penalty.
22 Yahweh ransoms the lives of those who
serve him,
and there will be no penalty for those
who take refuge in him.

PSALM 35

PRAYER OF THE VIRTUOUS IN PERSECUTION

Of David

1 Accuse my accusers, Yahweh,
attack my attackers.
2 Grasp your buckler and shield,
up, and help me.
3 Brandish spear and pike
to confront my pursuers,
give me the assurance, 'I am your Saviour.'

4 Shame and humiliation on those
who are out to kill me!

Defeat and repulse in dismay
　　on those who plot my downfall.

5 May they be like chaff before the wind,
　　with the angel of Yahweh to chase them.
6 May their way be dark and slippery,
　　with the angel of Yahweh to hound them.

7 Unprovoked they laid their snare for me,
　　unprovoked dug a trap to kill me.
8 Ruin comes upon them unawares;
　　the snare they have laid will catch them,
and into their own trap they will fall.

9 Then I shall delight in Yahweh,
　　rejoice that he has saved me.
10 My very bones will all exclaim,
　　Yahweh, who can compare with you
in rescuing the poor from the oppressor;
　　the needy from the exploiter?

11 False witnesses come forward against me
　　asking me questions I cannot answer,
they cross-examine me, 12repay my kindness with cruelty,
　　make my life barren.

13 But I, when they were ill, had worn sackcloth,
　　and mortified myself with fasting,

praying ever anew in my heart,

   ¹⁴ as if for a friend or brother; I had wandered restless,
      as if mourning a mother,
         so bowed had I been in sorrow.

¹⁵ When I stumble they gather in glee,
      gather around me;
   strangers I never even knew
      tear me apart incessantly.
¹⁶ If I fall they surround me,
      grinding their teeth at me.

¹⁷ How much longer, Lord, will you look on?
   Rescue me from their onslaughts,
      from young lions rescue the one life that I have.
¹⁸ I will give you thanks in the great assembly
   praise you where the people gather.

¹⁹ Let not my lying enemies
      gloat over me;
   those who hate me unprovoked
      look askance at me.

²⁰ They have no greeting of peace
      to the peace-loving people of the land;
   they think up deceptive speeches.
²¹ Their mouths wide open to accuse me,
      they say, 'Come on now, we saw you.'

²² You saw it, Yahweh, do not stay silent;
    Lord, do not stand aloof from me.
²³ Up, awake, to my defence,
    my God and my Lord, to my cause.
²⁴ In your saving justice give judgement for me,
    Yahweh my God,
        and do not let them gloat over me.

²⁵ Do not let them think, 'Just as we hoped,'
    nor, 'Now we have swallowed him up.'
²⁶ Shame and dismay on them all
    who gloat over my misfortunes.
  Let all who profit at my expense
    be covered with shame and disgrace.

²⁷ But let all who delight in my uprightness
    shout for joy and gladness;
  let them constantly say,
    'Great is Yahweh,
  who delights to see his servant in peace.'

²⁸ And my tongue shall recount your saving justice,
    all day long sing your praise.

PSALM 36

THE PERVERSITY OF SINNERS AND
THE BENEVOLENCE OF GOD

For the choirmaster   Of the servant of Yahweh   Of David

¹ Sin is the oracle of the wicked
     in the depths of his heart;
there is no fear of God
     before his eyes.

² He sees himself with too flattering an eye
     to detect and detest his guilt;
³ all he says is malicious and deceitful,
     he has turned his back on wisdom.

To get his way ⁴he hatches malicious plots
     even in his bed;
once set on his evil course
     no wickedness is too much for him.

⁵ Yahweh, your faithful love is in the heavens,
your constancy reaches to the clouds,
⁶ your saving justice is like towering mountains,
your judgements like the mighty deep.

Yahweh, you support both man and beast;
⁷ how precious, God, is your faithful love.

So the children of Adam
take refuge in the shadow of your wings.

8 They feast on the bounty of your house,
you let them drink from your delicious streams;
9 in you is the source of life,
by your light we see the light.

10 Maintain your faithful love to those who acknowledge
you,
and your saving justice to the honest of heart.
11 Do not let the foot of the arrogant overtake me
or wicked hands drive me away.

12 There they have fallen, the evil-doers,
flung down, never to rise again.

PSALM 37

THE FATE OF THE UPRIGHT AND THE WICKED

Of David

Aleph   1 Do not get heated about the wicked
or envy those who do wrong.
2 Quick as the grass they wither,
fading like the green of the fields.

Bet   3 Put your trust in Yahweh and do right,
         make your home in the land and live secure.
      4 Make Yahweh your joy
         and he will give you your heart's desires.

Gimel 5 Commit your destiny to Yahweh,
         be confident in him, and he will act,
      6 making your uprightness clear as daylight,
         and the justice of your cause as the noon.

Dalet 7 Stay quiet before Yahweh, wait longingly for him,
         do not get heated over someone who is
              making a fortune,
         succeeding by devious means.

He   8 Refrain from anger, leave rage aside,
         do not get heated—it can do no good;
      9 for evil-doers will be annihilated,
         while those who hope in Yahweh shall have
              the land for their own.

Waw   10 A little while and the wicked will be no more,
         however well you search for the place, the
              wicked will not be there;
      11 but the poor will have the land for their own
         to enjoy untroubled peace.

Zain 12 The wicked plots against the upright

and gnashes his teeth at him,
¹³ but Yahweh only laughs at his efforts,
knowing that his end is in sight.

Het   ¹⁴ Though the wicked draw his sword
and bend his bow to slaughter the honest
and bring down the poor and the needy,
¹⁵ his sword will pierce his own heart,
and his bow will be shattered.

Tet   ¹⁶ What little the upright possesses
outweighs all the wealth of the wicked;
¹⁷ for the weapons of the wicked shall be shattered,
while Yahweh supports the upright.

Yod   ¹⁸ The lives of the just are in Yahweh's care,
their birthright will endure for ever;
¹⁹ they will not be put to shame when bad times
come,
in time of famine they will have plenty.

Kaph   ²⁰ The wicked, enemies of Yahweh, will be
destroyed,
they will vanish like the green of the pasture,
they will vanish in smoke.

Lamed   ²¹The wicked borrows and will not repay,
but the upright is generous in giving;

²² those he blesses will have the land for their own,
and those he curses be annihilated.

Mem   ²³ Yahweh guides a strong man's steps and keeps
them firm;
and takes pleasure in him.
²⁴ When he trips he is not thrown sprawling,
since Yahweh supports him by the hand.

Nun   ²⁵ Now I am old, but ever since my youth
I never saw an upright person abandoned,
or the descendants of the upright forced to
beg their bread.
²⁶ The upright is always compassionate, always
lending,
so his descendants reap a blessing.

Samek   ²⁷ Turn your back on evil and do good,
you will have a home for ever,
²⁸ for Yahweh loves justice
and will not forsake his faithful.

Ain   Evil-doers will perish eternally,
the descendants of the wicked be annihilated,
²⁹ but the upright shall have the land for their
own,
there they shall live for ever.

Pe   ³⁰ Wisdom comes from the lips of the upright,
and his tongue speaks what is right;

³¹ the law of his God is in his heart,
   his foot will never slip.

Zade   ³² The wicked keeps a close eye on the upright,
   looking out for a chance to kill him;
³³ Yahweh will never abandon him to the
      clutches of the wicked,
   nor let him be condemned if he is tried.

Qoph   ³⁴ Put your hope in Yahweh, keep to his path,
   he will raise you up to make the land your
      own;
   you will look on while the wicked are
      annihilated.

Resh   ³⁵ I have seen the wicked exultant,
   towering like a cedar of Lebanon.
³⁶ When next I passed he was gone,
   I searched for him and he was nowhere to be
      found.

Shin   ³⁷ Observe the innocent, consider the honest,
   for the lover of peace will not lack children.
³⁸ But the wicked will all be destroyed together,
   and their children annihilated.

Taw   ³⁹ The upright have Yahweh for their Saviour,
   their refuge in times of trouble;

40 Yahweh helps them and rescues them,
    he will rescue them from the wicked,
    and save them because they take refuge in him.

PSALM 38

PRAYER IN DISTRESS

Psalm Of David In commemoration

1 Yahweh, do not correct me in anger,
    do not discipline me in wrath.
2 For your arrows have pierced deep into me,
    your hand has pressed down upon me.
3 Your indignation has left no part of me unscathed,
    my sin has left no health in my bones.

4 My sins stand higher than my head,
    they weigh on me as an unbearable weight.
5 I have stinking, festering wounds,
    thanks to my folly.
6 I am twisted and bent double,
    I spend my days in gloom.

7 My loins burn with fever,
    no part of me is unscathed.
8 Numbed and utterly crushed
    I groan in distress of heart.

⁹ Lord, all my longing is known to you,
  my sighing no secret from you,
¹⁰ my heart is throbbing, my strength has failed,
  the light has gone out of my eyes.

¹¹ Friends and companions shun my disease,
  even the dearest of them keep their distance.
¹² Those with designs on my life lay snares,
  those who wish me ill speak of violence
  and hatch treachery all day long.

¹³ But I hear nothing, as though I were deaf,
  as though dumb, saying not a word.
¹⁴ I am like the one who, hearing nothing,
  has no sharp answer to make.

¹⁵ For in you, Yahweh, I put my hope,
  you, Lord my God, will give answer.
¹⁶ I said, 'Never let them gloat over me,
  do not let them take advantage of me if my foot
    slips.'

¹⁷ There is no escape for me from falling,
  no relief from my misery.
¹⁸ But I make no secret of my guilt,
  I am anxious at the thought of my sin.

[19] There is no numbering those who oppose me without
cause,
no counting those who hate me unprovoked,
[20] repaying me evil for good,
slandering me for trying to do them good.

[21] Yahweh, do not desert me,
my God, do not stand aloof from me.
[22] Come quickly to my help,
Lord, my Saviour!

PSALM 39

INSIGNIFICANCE OF HUMAN BEINGS BEFORE GOD

For the choirmaster   For Jeduthun   Psalm   Of David

[1] I said, 'I will watch how I behave
so that I do not sin by my tongue.
I will keep a muzzle on my mouth
as long as any sinner is near.'
[2] I stayed dumb, silent, speechless,
but the sinner's prosperity redoubled my torment.

[3] My heart had been smouldering within me,
but at the thought of this it flared up
and the words came bursting out,

⁴ Yahweh, let me know my fate,
   how much longer I have to live.
   Show me just how frail I am.

⁵‘ Look, you have given me but a hand's breadth or two
        of life,
   the length of my life is as nothing to you.
   Every human being that stands on earth is a mere puff
        of wind,
⁶ every human being that walks only a shadow;
   a mere puff of wind is the wealth stored away—
   no knowing who will profit from it.'

⁷ So now, Lord, what am I to hope for?
   My hope is in you.
⁸ Save me from all my sins,
   do not make me the butt of fools.
⁹ I keep silence, I speak no more
   since you yourself have been at work.

¹⁰ Take your scourge away from me.
   I am worn out by the blows you deal me.
¹¹ You correct human beings by punishing sin,
   like a moth you eat away all their desires—
   a human being is a mere puff of wind.

¹² Yahweh, hear my prayer,
   listen to my cry for help,

do not remain deaf to my weeping.
For I am a stranger in your house,
a nomad like all my ancestors.
¹³ Turn away your gaze that I may breathe freely
before I depart and am no more!

PSALM 40

SONG OF PRAISE AND PRAYER FOR HELP

For the choirmaster   Of David   Psalm

¹ I waited, I waited for Yahweh,
then he stooped to me
and heard my cry for help.

² He pulled me up from the seething chasm,
from the mud of the mire.
He set my feet on rock,
and made my footsteps firm.

³ He put a fresh song in my mouth,
praise of our God.
Many will be awestruck at the sight,
and will put their trust in Yahweh.

⁴ How blessed are those
who put their trust in Yahweh,

who have not sided with rebels
and those who have gone astray in falsehood.

5 How much you have done,
Yahweh, my God—
your wonders, your plans for us—
you have no equal.
I will proclaim and speak of them;
they are beyond number.

6 You wanted no sacrifice or cereal offering,
but you gave me an open ear,
you did not ask for burnt offering or sacrifice for sin;
7 then I said, 'Here I am, I am coming.'

In the scroll of the book it is written of me,
8 my delight is to do your will;
your law, my God,
is deep in my heart.

9 I proclaimed the saving justice of Yahweh
in the great assembly.
See, I will not hold my tongue,
as you well know.

10 I have not kept your saving justice locked in the depths
of my heart,
but have spoken of your constancy and saving help.

I have made no secret of your faithful and steadfast love,
    in the great assembly.

[11] You, Yahweh, have not withheld
    your tenderness from me;
your faithful and steadfast love
    will always guard me.

[12] For troubles surround me,
    until they are beyond number;
my sins have overtaken me;
    I cannot see my way.
They outnumber the hairs of my head,
    and my heart fails me.

[13] Be pleased, Yahweh, to rescue me,[a]
    Yahweh, come quickly and help me!
[14] Shame and dismay to all
    who seek to take my life.

Back with them, let them be humiliated
    who delight in my misfortunes.
[15] Let them be aghast with shame,
    those who say to me, 'Aha, aha!'

[16] But joy and happiness in you
    to all who seek you!
Let them ceaselessly cry, 'Great is Yahweh'

who love your saving power.

[17] Poor and needy as I am,
  the Lord has me in mind.
You, my helper, my Saviour,
  my God, do not delay.

PSALM 41

PRAYER OF A SUFFERER DESERTED

For the choirmaster   Psalm   Of David

[1] Blessed is anyone who cares for the poor and the weak;
  in time of trouble Yahweh rescues him.
[2] Yahweh protects him, gives him life and happiness on
      earth.
  Do not abandon him to his enemies' pleasure!
[3] Yahweh sustains him on his bed of sickness;
  you transform altogether the bed where he lies sick.

[4] For my part I said, 'Yahweh, take pity on me!
  Cure me for I have sinned against you.'
[5] My enemies speak to me only of disaster,
' When will he die and his name disappear?'
[6] When people come to see me their talk is hollow,
  when they get out they spread the news with spite in
      their hearts.

7 All who hate me whisper together about me
   and reckon I deserve the misery I suffer.
8 A fatal sickness has a grip on him;
   now that he is down, he will never get up again.'
9 Even my trusted friend on whom I relied,
   who shared my table, takes advantage of me.

10 But you, Yahweh, take pity on me!
   Put me on my feet and I will give them their due.
11 This will convince me that you delight in me,
   if my enemy no longer exults over me.
12 Then you will keep me unscathed,
   and set me in your presence for ever.

13 Blessed be Yahweh, the God of Israel,
     from eternity to eternity.
        Amen, Amen.[a]

PSALM 42– 43

LAMENT OF A LEVITE IN EXILE

For the choirmaster   Poem   Of the sons of Korah

1 As a deer yearns
     for running streams,
   so I yearn
     for you, my God.

² I thirst for God,
    the living God;
when shall I go to see
    the face of God?

³ I have no food but tears
    day and night,
as all day long I am taunted,
    'Where is your God?'

⁴ This I remember
    as I pour out my heart,
how I used to pass under the roof of the Most High
    used to go to the house of God,
among cries of joy and praise,
    the sound of the feast.

⁵ Why be so downcast,
    why all these sighs?
Hope in God! I will praise him still,
    my Saviour, ⁶my God.

When I am downcast
    I think of you:
from the land of Jordan and Hermon,
    I think of you, humble mountain.

7 Deep is calling to deep
   by the roar of your cataracts,
all your waves and breakers
   have rolled over me.

8 In the daytime God sends his faithful love,
   and even at night;
the song it inspires in me
   is a prayer to my living God.

9 I shall say to God, my rock,
   'Why have you forgotten me?
Why must I go around in mourning,
   harrassed by the enemy?'

10 With death in my bones,
   my enemies taunt me,
all day long they ask me,
   'Where is your God?'

11 Why so downcast,
   why all these sighs?
Hope in God! I will praise him still,
   my Saviour, my God.

43

¹ Judge me, God, defend my cause
    against a people who have no faithful love;
from those who are treacherous and unjust,
    rescue me.

² For you are the God of my strength;
    why abandon me?
Why must I go around in mourning,
    harrassed by the enemy?

³ Send out your light and your truth;
    they shall be my guide,
to lead me to your holy mountain
    to the place where you dwell.

⁴ Then I shall go to the altar of God,
    to the God of my joy.
I will rejoice and praise you on the harp,
    O God, my God.

⁵ Why so downcast,
    why all these sighs?
Hope in God! I will praise him still,
    my Saviour, my God.

PSALM 44

NATIONAL LAMENT

For the choirmaster   Of the sons of Korah   Poem

¹ God, we have heard for ourselves,
   our ancestors have told us,
   of the deeds you did in their days,
   in days of old, ²by your hand.

To establish them in the land you drove out nations,
   to make room for them you harried peoples.
³ It was not their own sword that won the land,
   nor their own arms which made them victorious,
   but your hand it was and your arm,
   and the light of your presence, for you loved them.

⁴ You are my king, my God,
   who decreed Jacob's victories;
⁵ through you we conquered our opponents,
   in your name we trampled down those who rose up
         against us.

⁶ For my trust was not in my bow,
   my victory was not won by my sword;
⁷ it was you who saved us from our opponents,
   you who put to shame those who hate us.
⁸ Our boast was always of God,

we praised your name without ceasing.   *Pause*

9 Yet now you have abandoned and humiliated us,
   you no longer take the field with our armies,
10 you leave us to fall back before the enemy,
   those who hate us plunder us at will.

11 You hand us over like sheep for slaughter,
   you scatter us among the nations,
12 you sell your people for a trifle
   and make no profit on the sale.

13 You make us the butt of our neighbours,
   the mockery and scorn of those around us,
14 you make us a by-word among nations,
   other peoples shake their heads over us.

15 All day long I brood on my disgrace,
   the shame written clear on my face,
16 from the sound of insult and abuse,
   from the sight of hatred and vengefulness.

17 All this has befallen us though we had not forgotten you,
   nor been disloyal to your covenant,
18 our hearts never turning away,
   our feet never straying from your path.
19 Yet you have crushed us in the place where jackals live,
   and immersed us in shadow dark as death.

²⁰ Had we forgotten the name of our God
   and stretched out our hands to a foreign god,
²¹ would not God have found this out,
   for he knows the secrets of the heart?
²² For your sake we are being massacred all day long,
   treated as sheep to be slaughtered.

²³ Wake, Lord! Why are you asleep?
   Awake! Do not abandon us for good.
²⁴ Why do you turn your face away,
   forgetting that we are poor and harrassed?

²⁵ For we are bowed down to the dust,
   and lie prone on the ground.
²⁶ Arise! Come to our help!
   Ransom us, as your faithful love demands.

PSALM 45

ROYAL WEDDING SONG

*For the choirmaster   Tune: 'Lilies ...'   Of the sons of Korah
Poem   Love song*

¹ My heart is stirred by a noble theme,
   I address my poem to the king,
   my tongue the pen of an expert scribe.

² Of all men you are the most handsome,
  gracefulness is a dew upon your lips,
  or God has blessed you for ever.

³ Warrior, strap your sword at your side,
  in your majesty and splendour advance, ⁴ride on
  in the cause of truth, gentleness and uprightness.

  Stretch the bowstring tight, lending terror to your
      right hand.
⁵ Your arrows are sharp, nations lie at your mercy,
  the king's enemies lose heart.

⁶ Your throne is from God, for ever and ever,
  the sceptre of your kingship a sceptre of justice,
⁷ you love uprightness and detest evil.

  This is why God, your God, has anointed you
  with oil of gladness, as none of your rivals,
⁸ your robes all myrrh and aloes.

  From palaces of ivory, harps bring you joy,
⁹ in your retinue are daughters of kings,
  the consort at your right hand in gold of Ophir.

¹⁰ Listen, my daughter, attend to my words and hear;
   forget your own nation and your ancestral home,
¹¹ then the king will fall in love with your beauty;

he is your lord, bow down before him.
¹² The daughter of Tyre will court your favour with gifts,
and the richest of peoples ¹³with jewels set in gold.

Clothed ¹⁴in brocade, the king's daughter is led within
to the king with the maidens of her retinue;
her companions are brought to her,
¹⁵ they enter the king's palace with joy and rejoicing.
¹⁶Instead of your ancestors you will have sons;
you will make them rulers over the whole world.

¹⁷ I will make your name endure from generation to
generation,
so nations will sing your praise for ever and ever.

PSALM 46

GOD IS WITH US

For the choirmaster   Of the sons of Korah   For oboe   Song

¹ God is both refuge and strength for us,
a help always ready in trouble;
² so we shall not be afraid though the earth be in
turmoil,
though mountains tumble into the depths of the sea,
³ and its waters roar and seethe,
and the mountains totter as it heaves.

(Yahweh Sabaoth is with us,
our citadel, the God of Jacob.)   *Pause*

4 There is a river whose streams bring joy to God's city,
it sanctifies the dwelling of the Most High.
5 God is in the city, it cannot fall;
at break of day God comes to its rescue.
6 Nations are in uproar, kingdoms are tumbling,
when he raises his voice the earth crumbles away.

7Yahweh Sabaoth is with us,
our citadel, the God of Jacob.   *Pause*

8 Come, consider the wonders of Yahweh,
the astounding deeds he has done on the earth;
9 he puts an end to wars over the whole wide world,
he breaks the bow, he snaps the spear,
shields he burns in the fire.
10 Be still and acknowledge that I am God,
supreme over nations, supreme over the world.'

11 Yahweh Sabaoth is with us,
our citadel, the God of Jacob.   *Pause*

PSALM 47

YAHWEH KING OF ISRAEL, KING OF THE WORLD

For the choirmaster   Of the sons of Korah   Psalm

¹ Clap your hands, all peoples,
  acclaim God with shouts of joy.

² For Yahweh, the Most High, is glorious,
  the great king over all the earth.
³ He brings peoples under our yoke
  and nations under our feet.

⁴ He chooses for us our birthright,
  the pride of Jacob whom he loves.   *Pause*

⁵ God goes up to shouts of acclaim,
  Yahweh to a fanfare on the ram's horn.

⁶ Let the music sound for our God, let it sound,
  let the music sound for our king, let it sound.

⁷ For he is king of the whole world;
  learn the music, let it sound for God!
⁸ God reigns over the nations,
  seated on his holy throne.

[9]The leaders of the nations rally
to the people of the God of Abraham.
The shields of the earth belong to God,
who is exalted on high.

PSALM 48

ZION, THE MOUNTAIN OF GOD

Song Psalm Of the sons of Korah

[1] Great is Yahweh and most worthy of praise
     in the city of our God,
   the holy mountain, [2]towering in beauty,
     the joy of the whole world:

   Mount Zion in the heart of the north,
     the settlement of the great king;
[3] God himself among its palaces
     has proved himself its bulwark.

[4] For look, kings made alliance,
     together they advanced;
[5] without a second glance, when they saw,
     they panicked and fled away.

[6] Trembling seized them on the spot,
     pains like those of a woman in labour;

7 it was the east wind,
    that wrecker of ships from Tarshish.

8 What we had heard we saw for ourselves
    in the city of our God,
  in the city of Yahweh Sabaoth,
    which God has established for ever.   *Pause*

9 We reflect on your faithful love, God,
    in your temple!
10 Both your name and your praise, God,
    are over the whole wide world.

  Your right hand is full of saving justice,
    11 Mount Zion rejoices,
  the daughters of Judah delight
    because of your saving justice.

12 Go round Zion, walk right through her,
    count her bastions,
13 admire her walls,
    examine her palaces,

  to tell future generations
    14 that such is God;
  our God for ever and ever,
    he is our guide!

PSALM 49

THE FUTILITY OF WEALTH

For the choirmaster   Of the sons of Korah   Psalm

1. Hear this, all nations,
   listen, all who dwell on earth,
2. people high and low,
   rich and poor alike!

3. My lips have wisdom to utter,
   my heart good sense to whisper.
4. I listen carefully to a proverb,
   I set my riddle to the music of the harp.

5. Why should I be afraid in times of trouble?
   Malice dogs me and hems me in.
6. They trust in their wealth,
   and boast of the profusion of their riches.

7. But no one can ever redeem himself
   or pay his own ransom to God,
8. the price for himself is too high;
   it can never be ⁹that he will live on for ever
   and avoid the sight of the abyss.

10. For he will see the wise also die
    no less than the fool and the brute,

and leave their wealth behind for others.

11 For ever no home but their tombs,
their dwelling-place age after age,
though they gave their name to whole territories.

12 In prosperity people lose their good sense,
they become no better than dumb animals.
13 So they go on in their self-assurance,
right up to the end they are content with their lot.

Pause

14 They are penned in Sheol like sheep,
Death will lead them to pasture,
and those who are honest will rule over them.

In the morning all trace of them will be gone,
Sheol will be their home.
15 But my soul God will ransom
from the clutches of Sheol, and will snatch me up.

Pause

16 Do not be overawed when someone gets rich,
and lives in ever greater splendour;
17 when he dies he will take nothing with him,
his wealth will not go down with him.

18Though he pampered himself while he lived

—and people praise you for looking after yourself—
¹⁹ he will go to join the ranks of his ancestors,
who will never again see the light.

²⁰ In prosperity people lose their good sense,
they become no better than dumb animals.

PSALM 50

WORSHIP IN SPIRIT AND TRUTH

Psalm   Of Asaph

¹ The God of gods, Yahweh, is speaking,
from east to west he summons the earth.
² From Zion, perfection of beauty, he shines forth;
³ he is coming, our God, and will not be silent.

Devouring fire ahead of him,
raging tempest around him,
⁴ he summons the heavens from on high,
and the earth to judge his people.

⁵ 'Gather to me my faithful,
who sealed my covenant by sacrifice.'
⁶ The heavens proclaim his saving justice,
'God himself is judge.'   *Pause*

⁷ 'Listen, my people, I am speaking,

Israel, I am giving evidence against you,
I, God, your God.

⁸ 'It is not with your sacrifices that I find fault,
those burnt offerings constantly before me;
⁹ I will not accept any bull from your homes,
nor a single goat from your folds.

¹⁰ 'For all forest creatures are mine already,
the animals on the mountains in their thousands.
¹¹ I know every bird in the air,
whatever moves in the fields is mine.

¹² 'If I am hungry I shall not tell you,
since the world and all it holds is mine.
¹³ Am I to eat the flesh of bulls
or drink the blood of goats?

¹⁴ 'Let thanksgiving be your sacrifice to God,
fulfil the vows you make to the Most High;
¹⁵ then if you call to me in time of trouble
I will rescue you and you will honour me.'
¹⁶ But to the wicked, God says:

'What right have you to recite my statutes,
to take my covenant on your lips,
¹⁷ when you detest my teaching,
and thrust my words behind you?

¹⁸ 'You make friends with a thief as soon as you see one,
   you feel at home with adulterers,
¹⁹ your conversation is devoted to wickedness,
   and your tongue to inventing lies.

²⁰ 'You sit there, slandering your own brother,
   you malign your own mother's son.
²¹ You do this, and am I to say nothing?
   Do you think that I am really like you?
   I charge you, indict you to your face.

²² 'Think it out, you who forget God,
   or I will tear you apart without hope of a rescuer.
²³ Honour to me is a sacrifice of thanksgiving;
   to the upright I will show God's salvation.'

PSALM 51

A PRAYER OF CONTRITION

*For the choirmaster   Of David   When the prophet Nathan had
come to him because he had gone to Bathsheba*

¹ Have mercy on me, O God, in your faithful love,
   in your great tenderness wipe away my offences;
² wash me clean from my guilt,
   purify me from my sin.

³ For I am well aware of my offences,
   my sin is constantly in mind.
⁴ Against you, you alone, I have sinned,
   I have done what you see to be wrong,

   that you may show your saving justice when you
         pass sentence,
   and your victory may appear when you give
         judgement,
⁵ remember, I was born guilty,
   a sinner from the moment of conception.

⁶ But you delight in sincerity of heart,
   and in secret you teach me wisdom.
⁷ Purify me with hyssop till I am clean,
   wash me till I am whiter than snow.

⁸ Let me hear the sound of joy and gladness,
   and the bones you have crushed will dance.
⁹ Turn away your face from my sins,
   and wipe away all my guilt.

¹⁰ God, create in me a clean heart,
   renew within me a resolute spirit,
¹¹ do not thrust me away from your presence,
   do not take away from me your spirit of holiness.

¹² Give me back the joy of your salvation,

sustain in me a generous spirit.
13 I shall teach the wicked your paths,
    and sinners will return to you.

14 Deliver me from bloodshed, God, God of my salvation,
    and my tongue will acclaim your saving justice.
15 Lord, open my lips,
    and my mouth will speak out your praise.

16 Sacrifice gives you no pleasure,
    burnt offering you do not desire.
17 Sacrifice to God is a broken spirit,
    a broken, contrite heart you never scorn.

18 In your graciousness do good to Zion,
    rebuild the walls of Jerusalem.
19 Then you will delight in upright sacrifices,
    —burnt offerings and whole oblations—
    and young bulls will be offered on your altar.

PSALM 52

THE FATE OF CYNICS

*For the choirmaster   Poem   Of David   When Doeg the Edomite
went and warned Saul, 'David has gone to Abimelech's house'*

1 Why take pride in being wicked,
       you champion in villainy,

all day long ²plotting crime?
Your tongue is razor-sharp,
    you artist in perfidy.

³ You prefer evil to good,
    lying to uprightness.   *Pause*
⁴ You revel in destructive talk,
    treacherous tongue!

⁵That is why God will crush you,
    destroy you once and for all,
    snatch you from your tent,
uproot you from the land of the living.   *Pause*

⁶ The upright will be awestruck as they see it,
    they will mock him,
⁷ 'So much for someone who would not place
    his reliance in God,
but relied on his own great wealth,
    and made himself strong by crime.'

⁸ But I, like a flourishing olive tree
    in the house of God,
put my trust in God's faithful love,
    for ever and ever.

⁹ I shall praise you for ever
    for what you have done,

and shall trust in your name, so full of goodness,
in the presence of your faithful.

PSALM 53

THE FATE OF THE GODLESS

For the choirmaster   In sickness   Poem   Of David

¹ The fool has said in his heart,
    'There is no God!'
They are corrupt, vile and unjust,
    not one of them does right.

² God looks down from heaven
    at the children of Adam,
to see if a single one is wise,
    a single one seeks God.

³ All have proved faithless,
    all alike turned sour,
not one of them does right,
    not a single one.

⁴ Are they not aware, these evil-doers?
    They are devouring my people;
this is the bread they eat,
    and they never call upon God.

5 They will be gripped with fear,
    just where there is no need for fear,
  for God scatters the bones of him who besieges you;
      they are mocked because God rejects them.

6 Who will bring from Zion salvation for Israel?
  When God brings his people home,
    what joy for Jacob, what happiness for Israel!

PSALM 54

APPEAL TO GOD, THE JUST JUDGE

*For the choirmaster   On stringed instruments   Poem   Of David
When the Ziphites went to Saul and said, 'Is not David hiding with us?'*

1 God, save me by your name,
    in your power vindicate me.
2 God, hear my prayer,
    listen to the words I speak.

3 Arrogant men are attacking me,
    bullies hounding me to death,
    no room in their thoughts for God.   *Pause*

4 But now God is coming to my help,
    the Lord, among those who sustain me.
5 May their wickedness recoil on those who lie in wait
      for me.

Yahweh, in your constancy destroy them.

6 How gladly will I offer you sacrifice,
  and praise your name, for it is good,
7 for it has rescued me from all my troubles,
  and my eye has feasted on my enemies.

PSALM 55

PRAYER WHEN SLANDERED

For the choirmaster   For strings   Poem   Of David

1 God, hear my prayer,
     do not hide away from my plea,
2 give me a hearing, answer me,
     my troubles give me no peace.

  I shudder ³at the enemy's shouts,
     at the outcry of the wicked;
  they heap up charges against me,
     in their anger bring hostile accusations against me.

4 My heart writhes within me,
     the terrors of death come upon me,
5 fear and trembling overwhelm me,
     and shuddering grips me.

⁶ And I say,
'Who will give me wings like a dove,
to fly away and find rest?'
⁷ How far I would escape,
and make a nest in the desert!   *Pause*

⁸ I would soon find a refuge
from the storm of abuse,
from the ⁹destructive tempest, Lord,
from the flood of their tongues.

For I see violence
and strife in the city,
¹⁰ day and night they make their rounds
along the city walls,

Inside live malice and mischief,
¹¹ inside lives destruction,
tyranny and treachery never absent
from its central square.

¹² Were it an enemy who insulted me,
that I could bear;
if an opponent pitted himself against me,
I could turn away from him.

¹³ But you, a person of my own rank,
a comrade and dear friend,

¹⁴ to whom I was bound by intimate friendship
in the house of God!

May they recoil in disorder,
¹⁵ may death descend on them,
may they go down alive to Sheol,
since evil shares their home with them.

¹⁶ For my part, I appeal to God,
and Yahweh saves me;
¹⁷ evening, morning, noon,
I complain and I groan.

He hears my cry,
¹⁸ he ransoms me and gives me peace
from the feud against me,
for they are taking me to law.

¹⁹ But God will listen and will humble them,
he who has been enthroned from the beginning;
no change of heart for them,
for they do not fear God.

²⁰ They attack those at peace with them,
going back on their oaths;
²¹ though their mouth is smoother than butter,
enmity is in their hearts;
their words more soothing than oil,

yet sharpened like swords.

²² Unload your burden onto Yahweh
and he will sustain you;
never will he allow
the upright to stumble.

²³ You, God, will thrust them down
to the abyss of destruction,
men bloodthirsty and deceptive,
before half their days are spent.

For my part, I put my trust in you.

PSALM 56

TRUST IN GOD

For the choirmaster   Tune: 'The oppression of distant princes'
Of David   In a quiet voice When the Philistines seized him in Gath

¹ Take pity on me, God, as they harry me,
pressing their attacks home all day.
² Those who harry me lie in wait for me all day,
countless are those who attack me from the heights.

³ When I am afraid, I put my trust in you,
⁴ in God, whose word I praise,

in God I put my trust and have no fear,
what power has human strength over me?

5 All day long they carp at my words,
their only thought is to harm me,
6 they gather together, lie in wait and spy on my
movements,
as though determined to take my life.

7 Because of this crime reject them,
in your anger, God, strike down the nations.
8 You yourself have counted up my sorrows,
collect my tears in your wineskin.
9 Then my enemies will turn back
on the day when I call.

This I know, that God is on my side.
10 In God whose word I praise,
in Yahweh whose word I praise,
11 in God I put my trust and have no fear;
what can mortal man do to me?

12 I am bound by the vows I have made, God,
I will pay you the debt of thanks,
13 for you have saved my life from death
to walk in the presence of God,
in the light of the living.

PSALM 57

AMONG FEROCIOUS ENEMIES

*For the choirmaster   Tune: 'Do not destroy'   Of David   In a quiet
voice   When he escaped from Saul in the cave*

1 Take pity on me, God, take pity on me,
   for in you I take refuge,
   in the shadow of your wings I take refuge,
   until the destruction is past.

2 I call to God the Most High,
   to God who has done everything for me;
3 may he send from heaven and save me,
   and check those who harry me;   *Pause*
   may God send his faithful love and his constancy.

4 I lie surrounded by lions,
   greedy for human prey,
   their teeth are spears and arrows,
   their tongue a sharp sword.

5 Be exalted above the heavens, God!
   Your glory over all the earth!
6 They laid a snare in my path
   —I was bowed with care—
   they dug a pit ahead of me,
   but fell in it themselves.   *Pause*

7 My heart is ready, God,
   my heart is ready;
   I will sing, and make music for you.
8 Awake, my glory,
   awake, lyre and harp,
   that I may awake the Dawn.

9 I will praise you among the peoples, Lord,
   I will make music for you among nations,
10 for your faithful love towers to heaven,
   your constancy to the clouds.
11 Be exalted above the heavens, God!
   Your glory over all the earth!

PSALM 58

THE JUDGE OF EARTHLY JUDGES

For the choirmaster   Tune: 'Do not destroy   Of David   In a quiet voice

1 Divine as you are, do you truly give upright verdicts?
   do you judge fairly the children of Adam?
2 No! You devise injustice in your hearts,
   and with your hands you administer tyranny on the
      earth.

3 Since the womb they have gone astray, the wicked,
   on the wrong path since their birth, with their unjust
      verdicts.

⁴ They are poisonous as any snake,
  deaf as an adder that blocks its ears

⁵ so as not to hear the magician's music,
  however skilful his spells.

⁶ God, break the teeth in their mouths,
  snap off the fangs of these young lions, Yahweh.

⁷ May they drain away like water running to waste,
  may they wither like trampled grass,

⁸ like the slug that melts as it moves
  or a still-born child that never sees the sun.

⁹ Before they sprout thorns like the bramble,
  green or burnt up, may retribution whirl them away.

¹⁰ The upright will rejoice to see vengeance done,
  and will bathe his feet in the blood of the wicked.

¹¹ 'So', people will say, 'the upright does have a reward;
  there is a God to dispense justice on earth.'

PSALM 59

AGAINST THE WICKED

For the choirmaster   Tune: 'Do not destroy'   Of David   In a quiet voice   When Saul sent men to watch David's house in order to have him killed

¹ Rescue me from my enemies, my God,
  be my stronghold from my assailants,

² rescue me from evil-doers,
from men of violence save me.

³ Look at them, lurking to ambush me,
violent men are attacking me,
for no fault, no sin of mine, Yahweh, ⁴for no guilt,
they come running to take up position.

Wake up, stand by me and keep watch,
⁵ Yahweh, God of Sabaoth, God of Israel,
rise up, to punish all the nations,
show no mercy to all these malicious traitors.   *Pause*

⁶ Back they come at nightfall,
snarling like curs,
prowling through the town.

⁷ Look how they rant in speech
with swords on their lips,
'Who is there to hear us?'

⁸ For your part, Yahweh, you laugh at them,
you make mockery of all nations.
⁹ My strength, I keep my eyes fixed on you.

For my stronghold is God,
¹⁰ the God who loves me faithfully is coming to meet me,
God will let me feast my eyes on those who lie in wait
for me.

¹¹ Do not annihilate them, or my people may forget;
   shake them in your power, bring them low,
      Lord, our shield.

¹² Sin is in their mouths, sin on their lips,
   so let them be trapped in their pride
   for the curses and lies that they utter.

¹³ Destroy them in your anger, destroy them till they are
      no more,
   and let it be known that God is Master
   in Jacob and the whole wide world.   *Pause*

      ¹⁴ Back they come at nightfall,
         snarling like curs,
         prowling through the town,
¹⁵ scavenging for something to eat,
   growling unless they have their fill.

¹⁶ And so I will sing of your strength,
   in the morning acclaim your faithful love;
   you have been a stronghold for me,
   a refuge when I was in trouble.

¹⁷ My strength, I will make music for you,
   for my stronghold is God,
   the God who loves me faithfully.

PSALM 60

NATIONAL PRAYER AFTER DEFEAT

For the choirmaster   To the tune 'The decree is a lily'   In a quiet voice   Of David   To be learnt   When he was at war with Aram-Naharaim and Aram-Zobah, and Joab marched back to destroy twelve thousand Edomites in the Valley of Salt

1 God, you have rejected us, broken us,
    you were angry, come back to us!
2 You made the earth tremble, split it open;
    now mend the rifts, it is tottering still.

3 You have forced your people to drink a bitter draught,
    forced us to drink a wine that made us reel.
4 You gave a signal to those who fear you
    to let them escape out of range of the bow.   *Pause*

5 To rescue those you love,
    save with your right hand and answer us.

6 God has spoken from his sanctuary,
    'In triumph I will divide up Shechem,
    and share out the Valley of Succoth.

7 'Mine is Gilead, mine Manasseh,
    Ephraim the helmet on my head,
    Judah my commander's baton,

8 'Moab a bowl for me to wash in,
   on Edom I plant my sandal.
   Now try shouting "Victory!" over me, Philistia!'

9 Who will lead me against a fortified city,
   who will guide me into Edom,
10 if not you, the God who has rejected us?
   God, you no longer march with our armies.

11 Bring us help in our time of crisis,
   any human help is worthless.
12 With God we shall do deeds of valour,
   he will trample down our enemies.

PSALM 61

PRAYER OF AN EXILE

For the choirmaster   For strings   Of David

1 God, hear my cry,
   listen to my prayer.
2 From the end of the earth I call to you
   with fainting heart.
   Lead me to the high rock that stands far out of my
      reach.

3 For you are my refuge,
   a strong tower against the enemy.

⁴Let me stay in your tent for ever,
    taking refuge in the shelter of your wings!
5 For you, God, accept my vows,
    you grant me the heritage of those who fear your name.

    ⁶ Let the king live on and on,
        let his years continue age after age.
7 May his throne be always in God's presence,
    your faithful love and constancy watch over him.

    ⁸ Then I shall always sing to your name,
        day after day fulfilling my vows.

PSALM 62

HOPE IN GOD ALONE

For the choirmaster …   Jeduthun   Psalm   Of David

1 In God alone there is rest for my soul,
    from him comes my safety;
2 he alone is my rock, my safety,
    my stronghold so that I stand unshaken.

3 How much longer will you set on a victim,
    all together, intent on murder,
like a rampart already leaning over,
    a wall already damaged?
4 Trickery is their only plan,

deception their only pleasure,
with lies on their lips they pronounce a blessing,
with a curse in their hearts.   *Pause*

5 Rest in God alone, my soul!
    He is the source of my hope.
6 He alone is my rock, my safety,
    my stronghold, so that I stand unwavering.
7 In God is my safety and my glory,
    the rock of my strength.

In God is my refuge; 8trust in him,
    you people, at all times.
Pour out your hearts to him,
    God is a refuge for us.   *Pause*

9 Ordinary people are a mere puff of wind,
    important people a delusion;
set both on the scales together,
    and they are lighter than a puff of wind.

10 Put no trust in extortion,
    no empty hopes in robbery;
however much wealth may multiply,
    do not set your heart on it.

11 Once God has spoken,
    twice have I heard this:

Strength belongs to God,
  [12] to you, Lord, faithful love;
and you repay everyone as their deeds deserve.

PSALM 63

YEARNING FOR GOD

Psalm   Of David   When he was in the desert of Judah

[1] God, you are my God, I pine for you;
  my heart thirsts for you,
  my body longs for you,
  as a land parched, dreary and waterless.
[2] Thus I have gazed on you in the sanctuary,
  seeing your power and your glory.

[3] Better your faithful love than life itself;
  my lips will praise you.
[4] Thus I will bless you all my life,
  in your name lift up my hands.
[5] All my longings fulfilled as with fat and rich foods,
  a song of joy on my lips and praise in my mouth.

[6] On my bed when I think of you,
  I muse on you in the watches of the night,
[7] for you have always been my help;
  in the shadow of your wings I rejoice;

8 my heart clings to you,
  your right hand supports me.

9 May those who are hounding me to death
  go down to the depths of the earth,
10 given over to the blade of the sword,
   and left as food for jackals.
11 Then the king shall rejoice in God,
   all who swear by him shall gain recognition,
   for the mouths of liars shall be silenced.

PSALM 64

PUNISHMENT FOR SLANDERERS

For the choirmaster   Psalm   Of David

1 Listen, God, to my voice as I plead,
  protect my life from fear of the enemy;
2 hide me from the league of the wicked,
  from the gang of evil-doers.

3 They sharpen their tongues like a sword,
  aim their arrows of poisonous abuse,
4 shoot at the innocent from cover,
  shoot suddenly, with nothing to fear.

5 They support each other in their evil designs,
  they discuss how to lay their snares.

'Who will see us?' they say,

⁶ 'or will penetrate our secrets?'

He will do that, he who penetrates human nature to
its depths,

the depths of the heart.

⁷ God has shot them with his arrow,
sudden were their wounds.

⁸ He brings them down because of their tongue,
and all who see them shake their heads.

⁹ Everyone will be awestruck,
proclaim what God has done,
and understand why he has done it.

¹⁰ The upright will rejoice in Yahweh,
will take refuge in him,
and all the honest will praise him.

PSALM 65

THANKSGIVING HYMN

For the choirmaster   Psalm   Of David   Song

¹ Praise is rightfully yours,
God, in Zion.
Vows to you shall be fulfilled,
² for you answer prayer.

All humanity must come to you
   ³ with its sinful deeds.
Our faults overwhelm us,
   but you blot them out.

⁴ How blessed those whom you choose
   and invite to dwell in your courts.
We shall be filled with the good things of your house,
   of your holy temple.

⁵ You respond to us with the marvels of your saving
      justice,
   God our Saviour,
hope of the whole wide world,
   even the distant islands.

⁶ By your strength you hold the mountains steady,
   being clothed in power,
⁷ you calm the turmoil of the seas,
   the turmoil of their waves.

The nations are in uproar,
   in panic those who live at the ends of the earth;
⁸ your miracles bring shouts of joy
   to the gateways of morning and evening.

⁹ You visit the earth and make it fruitful,
   you fill it with riches;

the river of God brims over with water,
    you provide the grain.

To that end
[10] you water its furrows abundantly, level its ridges,
    soften it with showers and bless its shoots.

[11] You crown the year with your generosity,
    richness seeps from your tracks,
[12] the pastures of the desert grow moist,
    the hillsides are wrapped in joy,
[13] the meadows are covered with flocks,
    the valleys clothed with wheat;
they shout and sing for joy.

PSALM 66

CORPORATE PRAYER OF THANKSGIVING

For the choirmaster   *Song*   *Psalm*

[1] Acclaim God, all the earth,
[2] sing psalms to the glory of his name,
    glorify him with your praises,
[3] say to God, 'How awesome you are!

'Your achievements are the measure of your power,
    your enemies woo your favour,

⁴ all the earth bows down before you,
    sings psalms to you, sings psalms to your name.'   *Pause*

⁵ Come and see the marvels of God,
    his awesome deeds for the children of Adam:
⁶ he changed the sea into dry land,
    they crossed the river on foot.

So let us rejoice in him,
⁷ who rules for ever by his power;
    his eyes keep watch on the nations
    to forestall rebellion against him.   *Pause*

⁸ Nations, bless our God,
    let the sound of his praise be heard;
⁹ he brings us to life
    and keeps our feet from stumbling.

¹⁰ God, you have put us to the test,
    refined us like silver,
¹¹ let us fall into the net;
    you have put a heavy strain on our backs,
¹² let men ride over our heads;
    but now the ordeal by fire and water is over,
    you have led us out to breathe again.

¹³ I bring burnt offerings to your house,
    I fulfil to you my vows,

¹⁴ the vows that rose to my lips,
that I pronounced when I was in trouble.

¹⁵ I will offer you rich burnt offerings,
with the smoke of burning rams.
I will sacrifice to you bullocks and goats. *Pause*

¹⁶ Come and listen, all who fear God,
while I tell what he has done for me.

¹⁷ To him I cried aloud,
high praise was on my tongue.
¹⁸ Had I been aware of guilt in my heart,
the Lord would not have listened,
¹⁹ but in fact God did listen,
attentive to the sound of my prayer.

²⁰ Blessed be God
who has not turned away my prayer,
nor his own faithful love from me.

PSALM 67

HARVEST SONG

For the choirmaster   For strings   Psalm   Song

¹ May God show kindness and bless us,
and make his face shine on us. *Pause*

² Then the earth will acknowledge your ways,
  and all nations your power to save.

³ Let the nations praise you, God,
  let all the nations praise you.

⁴ Let the nations rejoice and sing for joy,
  for you judge the world with justice,
  you judge the peoples with fairness,
  you guide the nations on earth.   *Pause*

⁵ Let the nations praise you, God,
  let all the nations praise you.

⁶ The earth has yielded its produce;
  God, our God has blessed us.
⁷ May God continue to bless us,
  and be revered by the whole wide world.

PSALM 68

AN EPIC OF ISRAEL'S GLORY

For the choirmaster   Of David   Psalm   Song

¹ Let God arise, let his enemies scatter,
  let his opponents flee before him.
² You disperse them like smoke;

as wax melts in the presence of a fire,
so the wicked melt at the presence of God.

3 The upright rejoice in the presence of God,
delighted and crying out for joy.
4 Sing to God, play music to his name,
build a road for the Rider of the Clouds,
rejoice in Yahweh, dance before him.

5 Father of orphans, defender of widows,
such is God in his holy dwelling.
6 God gives the lonely a home to live in,
leads prisoners out into prosperity,
but rebels must live in the bare wastelands.

7 God, when you set out at the head of your people,
when you strode over the desert, 8the earth rocked,

Pause

the heavens pelted down rain at the presence of
God,
at the presence of God, the God of Israel.

9 God, you rained down a shower of blessings,
when your heritage was weary you gave it strength.
10 Your family found a home, which you
in your generosity provided for the humble.

11 The Lord gave a command,

the good news of a countless army.
¹² The chieftains of the army are in flight, in flight,
and the fair one at home is sharing out the spoils.

¹³ While you are at ease in the sheepfolds,
the wings of the Dove[a] are being covered with silver,
and her feathers with a sheen of green gold;
¹⁴ when Shaddai scatters the chieftains,
through her it snows[b] on the Dark Mountain.

¹⁵ A mountain of God, the mountain of Bashan!
a haughty mountain, the mountain of Bashan!
¹⁶ Why be envious, haughty mountains,
of the mountain God has chosen for his dwelling?
There God will dwell for ever.

¹⁷ The chariots of God are thousand upon thousand;
God has come from Sinai to the sanctuary.
¹⁸ You have climbed the heights, taken captives,
you have taken men as tribute, even rebels
that Yahweh God might have a dwelling-place.

¹⁹ Blessed be the Lord day after day,
he carries us along, God our Saviour. *Pause*

²⁰ This God of ours is a God who saves;
from Lord Yahweh comes escape from death;
²¹ but God smashes the head of his enemies,

the long-haired skull of the prowling criminal.

22 The Lord has said, 'I will bring them back from
   Bashan,
   I will bring them back from the depths of the sea,
23 so that you may bathe your feet in blood,
   and the tongues of your dogs feast on your enemies.'

24 Your processions, God, are for all to see,
   the processions of my God, of my king, to the
      sanctuary;
25 singers ahead, musicians behind,
   in the middle come girls, beating their drums.

26 In choirs they bless God,
   Yahweh, since the foundation of Israel.

27 Benjamin was there, the youngest in front,
   the princes of Judah in bright-coloured robes,
   the princes of Zebulun, the princes of Naphtali.

28 Take command, my God, as befits your power,
   the power, God, which you have wielded for us,
29 from your temple high above Jerusalem.
   Kings will come to you bearing tribute.

30 Rebuke the Beast of the Reeds,
   that herd of bulls, that people of calves,

who bow down with ingots of silver.
Scatter the people who delight in war.
³¹ From Egypt nobles will come,
Ethiopia will stretch out its hands to God.

³² Kingdoms of the earth, sing to God,
play for ³³the Rider of the Heavens, the primeval
     heavens.   *Pause*
There he speaks, with a voice of power!
³⁴ Acknowledge the power of God.

Over Israel his splendour, in the clouds his power.
³⁵ Awesome is God in his sanctuary.
He, the God of Israel,
gives strength and power to his people.

Blessed be God.

PSALM 69

LAMENT

For the choirmaster   Tune: 'Lilies …'   Of David

¹ Save me, God, for the waters
have closed in on my very being.

² I am sinking in the deepest swamp

and there is no firm ground.
I have stepped into deep water
and the waves are washing over me.

3 I am exhausted with calling out, my throat is hoarse,
my eyes are worn out with searching for my God.

4 More numerous than the hairs of my head
are those who hate me without reason.
Those who seek to get rid of me are powerful,
my treacherous enemies.
(Must I give back what I have never stolen?)

5 God, you know how foolish I am,
my offences are not hidden from you.

6 Those who hope in you must not be made fools of,
Yahweh Sabaoth, because of me!

Those who seek you must not be disgraced,
God of Israel, because of me!

7 It is for you I bear insults,
my face is covered with shame,
8 I am estranged from my brothers,
alienated from my own mother's sons;
9 for I am eaten up with zeal for your house,
and insults directed against you fall on me.

¹⁰ I mortify myself with fasting,
    and find myself insulted for it,
¹¹ I dress myself in sackcloth
    and become their laughing-stock,
¹² the gossip of people sitting at the gate,
    and the theme of drunkards' songs.

¹³ And so, I pray to you, Yahweh,
    at the time of your favour;
in your faithful love answer me,
    in the constancy of your saving power.

¹⁴ Rescue me from the mire before I sink in;
    so I shall be saved from those who hate me,
    from the watery depths.
¹⁵ Let not the waves wash over me,
    nor the deep swallow me up,
nor the pit close its mouth on me.

¹⁶ Answer me, Yahweh, for your faithful love is generous;
    in your tenderness turn towards me;
¹⁷ do not turn away from your servant,
    be quick to answer me, for I am in trouble.
¹⁸ Come to my side, redeem me,
    ransom me because of my enemies.

¹⁹ You know well the insults,
    the shame and disgrace I endure.

Every one of my oppressors is known to you.
²⁰ Insult has broken my heart past cure.
   I hoped for sympathy, but in vain,
   for consolers—not one to be found.

²¹ To eat they gave me poison,
   to drink, vinegar when I was thirsty.
²² May their own table prove a trap for them,
   and their abundance a snare;
²³ may their eyes grow so dim that they cannot see,
   all their muscles lose their strength.

²⁴ Vent your fury on them,
   let your burning anger overtake them.
²⁵ Reduce their encampment to ruin,
   and leave their tents untenanted,
²⁶ for hounding someone you had already stricken,
   for redoubling the pain of one you had wounded.

²⁷ Charge them with crime after crime,
   exclude them from your saving justice,
²⁸ erase them from the book of life,
   do not enrol them among the upright.

²⁹ For myself, wounded wretch that I am,
   by your saving power raise me up!

30 I will praise God's name in song,
   I will extol him by thanksgiving,
31 for this will please Yahweh more than an ox,
   than a bullock horned and hoofed.

32 The humble have seen and are glad.
   Let your courage revive, you who seek God.
33 For God listens to the poor,
   he has never scorned his captive people.
34 Let heaven and earth and seas,
   and all that stirs in them, acclaim him!

35 For God will save Zion,
   and rebuild the cities of Judah,
   and people will live there on their own land;
36 the descendants of his servants will inherit it,
   and those who love his name will dwell there.

PSALM 70

A CRY OF DISTRESS

For the choirmaster Of David In commemoration

1 Be pleased, God, to rescue me,
   Yahweh, come quickly and help me!
2 Shame and dismay to those
   who seek my life!

Back with them! Let them be humiliated
   who delight in my misfortunes.
3 Let them shrink away covered with shame,
   those who say to me, 'Aha, aha!'

4 But joy and happiness in you
   to all who seek you.
Let them ceaselessly cry, 'God is great',
   who love your saving power.

5 Poor and needy as I am,
   God, come quickly to me!
Yahweh, my helper, my Saviour,
   do not delay!

PSALM 71

A PRAYER IN OLD AGE

1 In you, Yahweh, I take refuge,
I shall never be put to shame.
2 In your saving justice rescue me, deliver me,
listen to me and save me.

3 Be a sheltering rock for me,
   always accessible;
you have determined to save me,
   for you are my rock, my fortress.

⁴ My God, rescue me from the clutches of the wicked,
   from the grasp of the rogue and the ruthless.

⁵ For you are my hope, Lord,
   my trust, Yahweh, since boyhood.
⁶ On you I have relied since my birth,
   since my mother's womb you have been my portion,
   the constant theme of my praise.

⁷ Many were bewildered at me,
   but you are my sure refuge.
⁸ My mouth is full of your praises,
   filled with your splendour all day long.

⁹ Do not reject me in my old age,
   nor desert me when my strength is failing,
¹⁰ for my enemies are discussing me,
   those with designs on my life are plotting together.

¹¹ 'Hound him down, for God has deserted him!
   Seize him, there is no one to rescue him.'
¹² God, do not stand aloof,
   my God, come quickly to help me.

¹³ Shame and ruin
      on those who slander me,
   may those intent on harming me
      be covered with insult and infamy.

¹⁴ As for me, my hope will never fade,
   I will praise you more and more.
¹⁵ My lips shall proclaim your saving justice,
   your saving power all day long.

¹⁶ I will come in the power of Yahweh
   to tell of your justice, yours alone.
¹⁷ God, you have taught me from boyhood,
   and I am still proclaiming your marvels.

   ¹⁸ Now that I am old and grey-haired,
      God, do not desert me,
   till I have proclaimed your strength
   to generations still to come,
   your power ¹⁹and justice to the skies.

   You have done great things,
      God, who is like you?
²⁰ You have shown me much misery and hardship,
      but you will give me life again,
   You will raise me up again from the depths of the earth,
²¹ prolong my old age, and comfort me again.

²² For my part, I will thank you on the lyre
      for your constancy, my God.
   I will play the harp in your honour,
      Holy One of Israel.

23 My lips sing for joy as I play to you,
    because you have redeemed me,
24 and all day long my tongue
    muses on your saving justice.
  Shame and disgrace
    on those intent to harm me!

PSALM 72

THE PROMISED KING

Of Solomon

1 God, endow the king with your own fair judgement,
    the son of the king with your own saving justice,
2 that he may rule your people with justice,
    and your poor with fair judgement.

3 Mountains and hills,
    bring peace to the people!
  With justice 4he will judge the poor of the people,
  he will save the children of the needy
    and crush their oppressors.

5 In the sight of the sun and the moon he will endure,
    age after age.
6 He will come down like rain on mown grass,
    like showers moistening the land.

⁷ In his days uprightness shall flourish,
and peace in plenty till the moon is no more.
⁸ His empire shall stretch from sea to sea,
from the river to the limits of the earth.

⁹ The Beast will cower before him,
his enemies lick the dust;
¹⁰ the kings of Tarshish and the islands
will pay him tribute.

The kings of Sheba and Saba
will offer gifts;
¹¹ all kings will do him homage,
all nations become his servants.

¹² For he rescues the needy who calls to him,
and the poor who has no one to help.
¹³ He has pity on the weak and the needy,
and saves the needy from death.

¹⁴ From oppression and violence he redeems their lives,
their blood is precious in his sight.
¹⁵ (Long may he live; may the gold of Sheba be given him!)
Prayer will be offered for him constantly,
and blessings invoked on him all day.

¹⁶ May wheat abound in the land,
waving on the heights of the hills,

like Lebanon with its fruits and flowers at their best,
like the grasses of the earth.

[17] May his name be blessed for ever,
and endure in the sight of the sun.
In him shall be blessed every race in the world,
and all nations call him blessed.

[18] Blessed be Yahweh, the God of Israel,
who alone works wonders;
[19] blessed for ever his glorious name.
May the whole world be filled with his glory!
Amen! Amen!

[20] End of the prayers of David, son of Jesse.

PSALM 73

THE TRIUMPH OF JUSTICE

Psalm   Of Asaph

[1] Indeed God is good to Israel,
the Lord to those who are pure of heart.

[2] My feet were on the point of stumbling,
a little more and I had slipped,
[3] envying the arrogant as I did,
and seeing the prosperity of the wicked.

⁴ For them no such thing as pain,
   untroubled, their comfortable portliness;
⁵ exempt from the cares which are the human lot,
   they have no part in Adam's afflictions.

⁶ So pride is a necklace to them,
   violence the garment they wear.
⁷ From their fat oozes out malice,
   their hearts drip with cunning.

⁸ Cynically they advocate evil,
   loftily they advocate force.
⁹ Their mouth claims heaven for themselves,
   and their tongue is never still on earth.

¹⁰ That is why my people turn to them,
   and enjoy the waters of plenty,
¹¹ saying, 'How can God know?
   What knowledge can the Most High have?'
¹² That is what the wicked are like,
   piling up wealth without any worries.

¹³ Was it useless, then, to have kept my own heart clean,
   to have washed my hands in innocence?

¹⁴ When I was under a hail of blows all day long,
   and punished every morning,
¹⁵ had I said, 'I shall talk like them,'

I should have betrayed your children's race.

¹⁶ So I set myself to understand this:
   how difficult I found it!
¹⁷ Until I went into the sanctuaries of the gods
   and understood what was destined to become of them.
¹⁸ You place them on a slippery slope
   and drive them down into chaos.

¹⁹ How sudden their hideous destruction!
   They are swept away, annihilated by terror!
²⁰ Like a dream upon waking, Lord,
   when you awake, you dismiss their image.

²¹ My heart grew embittered,
   my affections dried up,
²² I was stupid and uncomprehending,
   a clumsy animal in your presence.

²³ Even so, I stayed in your presence,
   you grasped me by the right hand;
²⁴you will guide me with advice,
   and will draw me in the wake of your glory.

²⁵ Who else is there for me in heaven?
   And, with you, I lack nothing on earth.
²⁶ My heart and my flesh are pining away:
   my heart's rock, my portion, God for ever!

²⁷ Truly, those who abandon you will perish;
  you destroy those who adulterously desert you,
²⁸ whereas my happiness is to be near God.
  I have made the Lord Yahweh my refuge,
  to tell of all your works.

PSALM 74

LAMENT ON THE SACK OF THE TEMPLE

Poem   Of Asaph

¹ God, why have you finally rejected us,
  your anger blazing against the flock you used to pasture?
² Remember the people you took to yourself long ago,
  your own tribe which you redeemed,
  and this Mount Zion where you came to live.

³ Come up to these endless ruins!
  The enemy have sacked everything in the sanctuary;
⁴ your opponents made uproar in the place of assemblies,
  they fixed their emblems over the entrance,
  emblems ⁵never known before.

  Their axes deep in the wood, ⁶hacking at the panels,
  they battered them down with axe and pick;
⁷ they set fire to your sanctuary,
  profanely rased to the ground the dwelling-place of
    your name.

8 They said to themselves, 'Let us crush them at one
    stroke!'
  They burned down every sacred shrine in the land.
9 We see no signs, no prophet any more,
  and none of us knows how long it will last.

10 How much longer, God, will the enemy blaspheme?
  Is the enemy to insult your name for ever?
11 Why hold back your hand,
  keep your right hand hidden in the folds of your robe?

12 Yet, God, my king from the first,
  author of saving acts throughout the earth,
13 by your power you split the sea in two,
  and smashed the heads of the monsters on the waters.

14 You crushed Leviathan'sᵃ heads,
  gave him as food to the wild animals.
15 You released the springs and brooks,
  and turned primordial rivers into dry land.

16 Yours is the day and yours the night,
  you caused sun and light to exist,
17 you fixed all the boundaries of the earth,
  you created summer and winter.

18 Remember, Yahweh, the enemy's blasphemy,
  a foolish people insults your name.

¹⁹ Do not surrender your turtledove to the beast;
  do not forget for ever the life of your oppressed people.

²⁰ Look to the covenant!
  All the hiding-places of the land are full,
    haunts of violence.
²¹ Do not let the downtrodden retreat in confusion,
  give the poor and needy cause to praise your name.

²² Arise, God, champion your own cause,
  remember how fools blaspheme you all day long!
²³ Do not forget the shouting of your enemies,
  the ever-mounting uproar of your adversaries.

PSALM 75

THE UNIVERSAL JUDGE

For the choirmaster   Tune: 'Do not destroy'   Psalm   Of Asaph
Song

¹ We give thanks to you, God, we give thanks to you,
   as we call upon your name, as we recount your
     wonders.

² 'At the appointed time
   I myself shall dispense justice.
³ The earth quakes and all its inhabitants;
   it is I who hold its pillars firm.   *Pause*

⁴ 'I said to the boastful, "Do not boast!"
  to the wicked, "Do not flaunt your strength!
⁵ Do not flaunt your strength so proudly,
  do not talk with that arrogant stance."'

⁶ No longer from east to west,
  no longer in the mountainous desert,
⁷ is God judging in uprightness,
  bringing some down, raising others.
⁸ Yahweh is holding a cup
  filled with a heady blend of wine;
  he pour it, they will drink it to the dregs,
  all the wicked on earth will drink it.

⁹ But I shall speak out for ever,
  shall make music for the God of Jacob.
¹⁰ I shall break down all the strength of the wicked,
  and the strength of the upright will rise high.

PSALM 76

HYMN TO GOD THE AWE-INSPIRING

For the choirmaster For strings Psalm Of Asaph Song

¹ God is acknowledged in Judah,
  his name is great in Israel,
² his tent is pitched in Salem,
  his dwelling is in Zion;

³ there he has broken the lightning-flashes of the bow,
shield and sword and war.   *Pause*

⁴ Radiant you are, and renowned
for the mountains of booty ⁵taken from them.
Heroes are now sleeping their last sleep,
the warriors' arms have failed them;
⁶ at your reproof, God of Jacob,
chariot and horse stand stunned.

⁷ You, you alone, strike terror! Who can hold his ground
in your presence when your anger strikes?
⁸ From heaven your verdicts thunder,
the earth is silent with dread
⁹ when God takes his stand to give judgement,
to save all the humble of the earth.   *Pause*

¹⁰ Human anger serves only to praise you,
the survivors of your anger will huddle round you.
¹¹ Make and fulfil your vows to Yahweh your God,
let those who surround him make offerings to the
Awesome One.
¹² He cuts short the breath of princes,
strikes terror in earthly kings.

PSALM 77

MEDITATION ON ISRAEL'S PAST

For the choirmaster ...   Jeduthun   Of Asaph   Psalm

¹ I cry to God in distress,
  I cry to God and he hears me.

² In the day of my distress I sought the Lord;
  all night I tirelessly stretched out my hands,
  my heart refused to be consoled.
³ I sigh as I think of God,
  my spirit faints away as I ponder on him.   *Pause*

⁴ You kept me from closing my eyes,
  I was too distraught to speak;
⁵ I thought of former times,
  years long past ⁶I recalled;
  through the night I ponder in my heart,
  as I reflect, my spirit asks this question:

⁷ Is the Lord's rejection final?
  Will he never show favour again?
⁸ Is his faithful love gone for ever?
  Has his Word come to an end for all time?
⁹ Does God forget to show mercy?
  In anger does he shut off his tenderness?   *Pause*

¹⁰ And I said, 'This is what wounds me,
   the right hand of the Most High has lost its strength.'
¹¹ Remembering Yahweh's great deeds,
   remembering your wonders in the past,
¹² I reflect on all that you did,
   I ponder all your great deeds.

¹³ God, your ways are holy!
   What god is as great as our God?
¹⁴ You are the God who does marvellous deeds,
   brought nations to acknowledge your power,
¹⁵ with your own arm redeeming your people,
   the children of Jacob and Joseph.   *Pause*

¹⁶ When the waters saw you, God,
   when the waters saw you they writhed in anguish,
   the very depths shook with fear.
¹⁷ The clouds pelted down water,
   the sky thundered,
   your arrows shot back and forth.

¹⁸ The rolling of your thunder was heard,
   your lightning-flashes lit up the world,
   the earth shuddered and shook.
¹⁹ Your way led over the sea,
   your path over the countless waters,
   and none could trace your footsteps.

²⁰ You guided your people like a flock
  by the hand of Moses and Aaron.

PSALM 78

THE LESSONS OF ISRAELITE HISTORY

Psalm   Of Asaph

¹ My people, listen to my teaching,
  pay attention to what I say.
² I will speak to you in poetry,
  unfold the mysteries of the past.

³ What we have heard and know,
  what our ancestors have told us
⁴ we shall not conceal from their descendants,
  but will tell to a generation still to come:

  the praises of Yahweh, his power,
  the wonderful deeds he has done.
⁵ He instituted a witness in Jacob,
  he established a law in Israel,

  he commanded our ancestors
  to hand it down to their descendants,
⁶ that a generation still to come might know it,
  children yet to be born.

They should be sure to tell their own children,
7 and should put their trust in God,
never forgetting God's great deeds,
always keeping his commands,

8 and not, like their ancestors,
be a stubborn and rebellious generation,
a generation weak of purpose,
their spirit fickle towards God.

9 The archer sons of Ephraim
turned tail when the time came for fighting;
10 they failed to keep God's covenant,
they refused to follow his Law;

11 they had forgotten his great deeds,
the marvels he had shown them;
12 he did marvels in the sight of their ancestors
in Egypt, in the plains of Tanis.

13 He split the sea and brought them through,
made the waters stand up like a dam;
14 he led them with a cloud by day,
and all the night with the light of a fire;

15 he split rocks in the desert,
let them drink as though from the limitless depths;
16 he brought forth streams from a rock,

made waters flow down in torrents.

¹⁷ But they only sinned against him more than ever,
  defying the Most High in barren country;
¹⁸ they deliberately challenged God
  by demanding food to their hearts' content.

¹⁹ They insulted God by saying,
  'Can God make a banquet in the desert?
²⁰ True, when he struck the rock,
  waters gushed out and flowed in torrents;
  but what of bread? Can he give that,
  can he provide meat for his people?'

²¹ When he heard them Yahweh vented his anger,
  fire blazed against Jacob,
  his anger mounted against Israel,
²² because they had no faith in God,
  no trust in his power to save.

²³ Even so he gave orders to the skies above,
  he opened the sluice-gates of heaven;
²⁴ he rained down manna to feed them,
  he gave them the wheat of heaven;
²⁵ mere mortals ate the bread of the Mighty,
  he sent them as much food as they could want.

²⁶ He roused an east wind in the heavens,

despatched a south wind by his strength;
27 he rained down meat on them like dust,
birds thick as sand on the seashore,
28 tumbling into the middle of his camp,
all around his dwelling-place.

29 They ate as much food as they wanted,
he satisfied all their cravings;
30 but their cravings were still upon them,
the food was still in their mouths,
31 when the wrath of God attacked them,
slaughtering their strongest men,
laying low the flower of Israel.

32 Despite all this, they went on sinning,
they put no faith in his marvels.
33 He made their days vanish in mist,
their years in sudden ruin.

34 Whenever he slaughtered them, they began to seek him,
they turned back and looked eagerly for him,
35 recalling that God was their rock,
God the Most High, their redeemer.

36 They tried to hoodwink him with their mouths,
their tongues were deceitful towards him;
37 their hearts were not loyal to him,
they were not faithful to his covenant.

38 But in his compassion he forgave their guilt
   instead of killing them,
   time and again repressing his anger
   instead of rousing his full wrath,
39 remembering they were creatures of flesh,
   a breath of wind that passes, never to return.

40 How often they defied him in the desert!
   How often they grieved him in the wastelands!
41 Repeatedly they challenged God,
   provoking the Holy One of Israel,
42 not remembering his hand,
   the time when he saved them from the oppressor,

43 he who did his signs in Egypt,
   his miracles in the plains of Tanis,
44 turning their rivers to blood,
   their streams so that they had nothing to drink.

45 He sent horseflies to eat them up,
   and frogs to devastate them,
46 consigning their crops to the caterpillar,
   the fruit of their hard work to the locust;

47 he killed their vines with hail,
   their sycamore trees with frost,
48 delivering up their cattle to hail,
   and their flocks to thunderbolts.

⁴⁹ He loosed against them the full heat of his anger,
fury, rage and destruction,
a detachment of destroying angels;
⁵⁰ he gave free course to his anger.

He did not exempt their own selves from death,
delivering up their lives to the plague.
⁵¹ He struck all the first-born in Egypt,
the flower of the youth in the tents of Ham.

⁵² He brought out his people like sheep,
guiding them like a flock in the desert,
⁵³ leading them safe and unafraid,
while the sea engulfed their enemies.

⁵⁴ He brought them to his holy land,
the hill-country won by his right hand;
⁵⁵ he dispossessed nations before them,
measured out a heritage for each of them,
and settled the tribes of Israel in their tents.

⁵⁶ But still they challenged the Most High God and
defied him,
r efusing to keep his decrees;
⁵⁷ as perverse and treacherous as their ancestors,
they gave way like a faulty bow,
⁵⁸ provoking him with their high places,
rousing his jealousy with their idols.

59 God listened and vented his wrath,
   he totally rejected Israel;
60 he forsook his dwelling in Shiloh,
   the tent where he used to dwell on the earth.

61 He abandoned his power to captivity,
   his splendour to the enemy's clutches;
62 he gave up his people to the sword,
   he vented his wrath on his own heritage.

63 Fire devoured their young men,
   their young girls had no wedding-song;
64 their priests fell by the sword
   and their widows sang no dirge.

65 The Lord arose as though he had been asleep,
   like a strong man fighting-mad with wine,
66 he struck his enemies on the rump,
   and put them to everlasting shame.

67 Rejecting the tents of Joseph,
   passing over the tribe of Ephraim,
68 he chose the tribe of Judah,
   his well-loved mountain of Zion;
69 he built his sanctuary like high hills,
   like the earth set it firm for ever.

70 He chose David to be his servant,

took him from the sheepfold,
⁷¹ took him from tending ewes
to pasture his servant Jacob,
and Israel his heritage.
⁷² He pastured them with unblemished heart,
with a sensitive hand he led them.

PSALM 79

NATIONAL LAMENT

Psalm   Of Asaph

¹ God, the pagans have invaded your heritage,
they have defiled your holy temple,
they have laid Jerusalem in ruins,
² they have left the corpses of your servants
as food for the birds of the air,
the bodies of your faithful for the wild beasts.

³ Around Jerusalem they have shed blood like water,
leaving no one to bury them.
⁴ We are the scorn of our neighbours,
the butt and laughing-stock of those around us.
⁵ How long will you be angry, Yahweh? For ever?
Is your jealousy to go on smouldering like a fire?

⁶ Pour out your anger on the nations
who do not acknowledge you,

and on the kingdoms
    that do not call on your name;
⁷ for they have devoured Jacob
    and devastated his home.

⁸ Do not count against us the guilt of former generations,
  in your tenderness come quickly to meet us,
  for we are utterly weakened;
⁹ help us, God our Saviour,
  for the glory of your name;
  Yahweh, wipe away our sins,
  rescue us for the sake of your name.

¹⁰ Why should the nations ask,
  'Where is their God?'
  Let us see the nations suffer vengeance
  for shedding your servants' blood.
¹¹ May the groans of the captive reach you,
  by your great strength save those who are condemned
    to death!

¹² Repay our neighbours sevenfold
  for the insults they have levelled at you, Lord.
¹³ And we, your people, the flock that you pasture,
  will thank you for ever,
  will recite your praises from age to age.

PSALM 80

PRAYER FOR THE RESTORATION OF ISRAEL

For the choirmaster   Tune: 'The decrees are lilies'   Of Asaph   Psalm

¹ Shepherd of Israel, listen,
  you who lead Joseph like a flock,
  enthroned on the winged creatures, shine forth
² over Ephraim, Benjamin and Manasseh;
  rouse your valour
  and come to our help.

³ God, bring us back,
  let your face shine on us and we shall be safe.

⁴ Yahweh, God Sabaoth, how long
  will you flare up at your people's prayer?
⁵ You have made tears their food,
  redoubled tears their drink.
⁶ You let our neighbours quarrel over us,
  our enemies mock us.

⁷ God Sabaoth, bring us back,
  let your face shine on us and we shall be safe.

⁸ You brought a vine out of Egypt,
  to plant it you drove out nations;

⁹ you cleared a space for it,
   it took root and filled the whole country.

¹⁰ The mountains were covered with its shade,
    and the cedars of God with its branches,
¹¹ its boughs stretched as far as the sea,
    its shoots as far as the River.

¹² Why have you broken down its fences?
    Every passer-by plucks its grapes,
¹³ boars from the forest tear at it,
    wild beasts feed on it.

¹⁴ God Sabaoth, come back, we pray,
    look down from heaven and see,
    visit this vine;
¹⁵ protect what your own hand has planted.
¹⁶ They have thrown it on the fire like dung,
    the frown of your rebuke will destroy them.

¹⁷ May your hand protect those at your side,
    the child of Adam you have strengthened for yourself!
¹⁸ Never again will we turn away from you,
    give us life and we will call upon your name.

¹⁹ God Sabaoth, bring us back,
    let your face shine on us and we shall be safe.

PSALM 81

FOR THE FEAST OF SHELTERS

For the choirmaster   On the … of Gath   Of Asaph

1 Sing for joy to God our strength,
  shout in triumph to the God of Jacob.

2 Strike up the music, beat the tambourine,
  play the melodious harp and the lyre;
3 blow the trumpet for the new month,
  for the full moon, for our feast day!

4 For Israel has this statute,
  a decision of the God of Jacob,
5 a decree he imposed on Joseph,
  when he went to war against Egypt.

  I heard a voice unknown to me,
6 'I freed his shoulder from the burden,
  his hands were able to lay aside the labourer's basket.
7 You cried out in your distress, so I rescued you.

  'Hidden in the storm, I answered you,
  I tested you at the waters of Meribah.   *Pause*
8 Listen, my people, while I give you warning;
  Israel, if only you would listen to me!

⁹‘ You shall have no strange gods,
   shall worship no alien god.
¹⁰ I, Yahweh, am your God,
   who brought you here from Egypt,
   you have only to open your mouth for me to fill it.

¹¹ ‘My people would not listen to me,
    Israel would have none of me.
¹² So I left them to their stubborn selves,
   to follow their own devices.

¹³ ‘If only my people would listen to me,
    if only Israel would walk in my ways,
¹⁴ at one stroke I would subdue their enemies,
   turn my hand against their opponents.

¹⁵ ‘Those who hate Yahweh would woo his favour,
    though their doom was sealed for ever,
¹⁶ while I would feed him on pure wheat,
   would give you your fill of honey from the rock.’

PSALM 82

AGAINST THE JUDGES OF THE NATIONS

Psalm   Of Asaph

¹ God takes his stand in the divine assembly,
   surrounded by the gods he gives judgement.

2 'How much longer will you give unjust judgements
   and uphold the prestige of the wicked?
3 Let the weak and the orphan have justice,
   be fair to the wretched and the destitute. *Pause*

4 'Rescue the weak and the needy,
   save them from the clutches of the wicked.

5 'Ignorant and uncomprehending, they wander in
      darkness,
   while the foundations of the world are tottering.
6 I had thought, "Are you gods,
   are all of you sons of the Most High?"
7 No! you will die as human beings do,
   as one man, princes, you will fall.'
8 Arise, God, judge the world,
   for all nations belong to you.

PSALM 83

AGAINST THE ENEMIES OF ISRAEL

Song   Psalm   Of Asaph

1 God, do not remain silent,
   do not stay quiet or unmoved, God!
2 See how your enemies are in uproar,
   how those who hate you are rearing their heads.

³ They are laying plans against your people,
  conspiring against those you cherish;
⁴ they say, 'Come, let us annihilate them as a nation,
  the name of Israel shall be remembered no more!'

⁵ They conspire with a single mind,
  they conclude an alliance against you,
⁶ the tents of Edom and the Ishmaelites,
  Moab and the Hagrites,
⁷ Gebal, Ammon, Amalek,
  Philistia and the Tyrians;
⁸ even Assyria has joined them
  to reinforce the children of Lot.   *Pause*

⁹ Treat them like Midian and Sisera,
  like Jabin at the river Kishon;
¹⁰ wiped out at En-Dor,
  they served to manure the ground.
¹¹ Treat their leaders like Oreb and Zeeb,
  all their commanders like Zebah and Zalmunna,
¹² for they said, 'Let us take for ourselves
  God's settlements.'

¹³ My God, treat them like thistledown,
  like chaff at the mercy of the wind.
¹⁴ As fire devours a forest,
  as a flame sets mountains ablaze,
¹⁵ so drive them away with your tempest,

by your whirlwind fill them with terror.
[16] Shame written all over their faces,
let them seek your name, Yahweh!
[17] Dishonour and terror be always theirs,
death also and destruction.
[18] Let them know that you alone bear the name of
Yahweh,
Most High over all the earth.

PSALM 84

PILGRIMAGE SONG

For the choirmaster   On the ... of Gath   Of the sons of Korah   Psalm

[1] How lovely are your dwelling-places,
Yahweh Sabaoth.
[2] My whole being yearns and pines
for Yahweh's courts,
My heart and my body cry out for joy
to the living God.

[3] Even the sparrow has found a home,
the swallow a nest to place its young:
your altars, Yahweh Sabaoth,
my King and my God.

[4] How blessed are those who live in your house;
they shall praise you continually.   *Pause*

⁵ Blessed those who find their strength in you,
  whose hearts are set on pilgrimage.
⁶ As they pass through the Valley of the Balsam,
  they make there a water-hole,
  and—a further blessing—early rain fills it.
⁷ They make their way from height to height,
  God shows himself to them in Zion.

⁸ Yahweh, God Sabaoth, hear my prayer,
  listen, God of Jacob.
⁹ God, our shield, look,
  and see the face of your anointed.

¹⁰ Better one day in your courts
      than a thousand at my own devices,
  to stand on the threshold of God's house
      than to live in the tents of the wicked.

¹¹ For Yahweh God is a rampart and shield,
      he gives grace and glory;
  Yahweh refuses nothing good
      to those whose life is blameless.

¹² Yahweh Sabaoth,
      blessed is he who trusts in you.

PSALM 85

PRAYER FOR PEACE AND JUSTICE

For the choirmaster   Of the sons of Korah   Psalm

1 Yahweh, you are gracious to your land,
  you bring back the captives of Jacob,
2 you take away the guilt of your people,
  you blot out all their sin.   *Pause*

3 You retract all your anger,
  you renounce the heat of your fury.

4 Bring us back, God our Saviour,
  appease your indignation against us!
5 Will you be angry with us for ever?
  Will you prolong your wrath age after age?

6 Will you not give us life again,
  for your people to rejoice in you?
7 Show us, Lord, your faithful love,
  grant us your saving help.

8 I am listening. What is God's message?
  Yahweh's message is peace
  for his people, for his faithful,
  if only they renounce their folly.
9 His saving help is near for those who fear him,

his glory will dwell in our land.

10 Faithful Love and Loyalty join together,
Saving Justice and Peace embrace.
11 Loyalty will spring up from the earth,
and Justice will lean down from heaven.

12 Yahweh will himself give prosperity,
and our soil will yield its harvest.
13 Justice will walk before him,
treading out a path.

PSALM 86

PRAYER IN TIME OF TRIAL

Prayer   Of David

1 Listen to me, Yahweh, answer me,
for I am poor and needy.
2 Guard me, for I am faithful,
save your servant who relies on you.

You are my God, 3take pity on me, Lord,
for to you I cry all the day.
4 Fill your servant's heart with joy, Lord,
for to you I raise up my heart.

⁵ Lord, you are kind and forgiving,
   rich in faithful love for all who call upon you.
⁶ Yahweh, hear my prayer,
   listen to the sound of my pleading.

⁷ In my day of distress I call upon you,
   because you answer me, Lord;
⁸ among the gods there is none to compare with you,
   no great deeds to compare with yours.

⁹ All nations will come and adore you, Lord,
   and give glory to your name.
¹⁰ For you are great and do marvellous deeds,
   you, God, and none other.

¹¹ Teach me, Yahweh, your ways,
   that I may not stray from your loyalty;
   let my heart's one aim be to fear your name.

¹² I thank you with all my heart, Lord my God,
   I will glorify your name for ever,
¹³ for your faithful love for me is so great
   that you have rescued me from the depths of Sheol.

¹⁴ Arrogant men, God, are rising up against me,
   a brutal gang is after my life,
   in their scheme of things you have no place.

¹⁵ But you, Lord, God of tenderness and mercy,
slow to anger, rich in faithful love and loyalty,
¹⁶ turn to me and pity me.

Give to your servant your strength,
to the child of your servant your saving help,
¹⁷ give me a sign of your kindness.

¹⁸ My enemies will see to their shame
that you, Yahweh, help and console me.

PSALM 87

ZION, MOTHER OF NATIONS

Of the sons of Korah   Psalm   Song

¹ With its foundations on the holy mountains,
² Yahweh loves his city,
he prefers the gates of Zion
to any dwelling-place in Jacob.

³ He speaks of glory for you,
city of God,   *Pause*

⁴ 'I number Rahab and Babylon
among those that acknowledge me;
look at Tyre, Philistia, Ethiopia,
so and so was born there.'

⁵ But of Zion it will be said,
  'Every one was born there,'
  her guarantee is the Most High.

⁶ Yahweh in his register of peoples
  will note against each, 'Born there',   *Pause*
⁷ princes no less than native-born;
  all make their home in you.

PSALM 88

PRAYER IN GREAT DISTRESS

*Song   Psalm Of the sons of Korah   In sickness   In suffering
Poem   For Heman the native-born*

¹ Yahweh, God of my salvation,
  when I cry out to you in the night,
² may my prayer reach your presence,
  hear my cry for help.

³ For I am filled with misery,
  my life is on the brink of Sheol;
⁴ already numbered among those who sink into oblivion,
  I am as one bereft of strength,
⁵ left alone among the dead,
  like the slaughtered lying in the grave,
  whom you remember no more,
  cut off as they are from your protection.

⁶ You have plunged me to the bottom of the grave,
  in the darkness, in the depths;
⁷ weighted down by your anger,
  kept low by your waves.   *Pause*

⁸ You have deprived me of my friends,
  made me repulsive to them,
  imprisoned, with no escape;
⁹ my eyes are worn out with suffering.
  I call to you, Yahweh, all day,
  I stretch out my hands to you.

¹⁰ Do you work wonders for the dead,
   can shadows rise up to praise you?   *Pause*
¹¹ Do they speak in the grave of your faithful love,
   of your constancy in the place of perdition?
¹² Are your wonders known in the darkness,
   your saving justice in the land of oblivion?

¹³ But, for my part, I cry to you, Yahweh,
   every morning my prayer comes before you;
¹⁴ why, Yahweh, do you rebuff me,
   turn your face away from me?

¹⁵ Wretched and close to death since childhood,
   I have borne your terrors—I am finished!
¹⁶ Your anger has overwhelmed me,
   your terrors annihilated me.

¹⁷ They flood around me all day long,
   close in on me all at once.
¹⁸ You have deprived me of friends and companions,
   and all that I know is the dark.

PSALM 89

HYMN AND PRAYER TO GOD THE FAITHFUL

Poem   For Ethan the native-born

¹ I shall sing the faithful love of Yahweh for ever,
   from age to age my lips shall declare your constancy,
² for you have said: love is built to last for ever,
   you have fixed your constancy firm in the heavens.

³ 'I have made a covenant with my Chosen One,
   sworn an oath to my servant David:
⁴ I have made your dynasty firm for ever,
   built your throne stable age after age.'   *Pause*

⁵ The heavens praise your wonders, Yahweh,
   your constancy in the gathering of your faithful.
⁶ Who in the skies can compare with Yahweh?
   Who among the sons of god can rival him?

⁷ God, awesome in the assembly of holy ones,
   great and dreaded among all who surround him,

⁸ Yahweh, God Sabaoth, who is like you?
    Mighty Yahweh, your constancy is all round you!

⁹ You control the pride of the ocean,
    when its waves ride high you calm them.
¹⁰ You split Rahabᵃ in two like a corpse,
    scattered your enemies with your mighty arm.

¹¹ Yours are the heavens and yours the earth,
    the world and all it holds, you founded them;
¹² you created the north and the south,
    Tabor and Hermon hail your name with joy.

¹³ Yours is a strong arm,
    mighty your hand, your right hand raised high;
¹⁴ Saving Justice and Fair Judgement the foundations of
        your throne,
    Faithful Love and Constancy march before you.

¹⁵ How blessed the nation that learns to acclaim you!
    They will live, Yahweh, in the light of your presence.
    ¹⁶ In your name they rejoice all day long,
        by your saving justice they are raised up.

¹⁷ You are the flower of their strength,
    by your favour our strength is triumphant;
¹⁸ for to Yahweh belongs our shield,
    to the Holy One of Israel our king.

¹⁹ Once you spoke in a vision,
  to your faithful you said:
‘ I have given strength to a warrior,
  I have raised up a man chosen from my people.

²⁰ ‘I have found David my servant,
  and anointed him with my holy oil.
²¹ My hand will always be with him,
  my arm will make him strong.

²² ‘No enemy will be able to outwit him,
  no wicked man overcome him;
²³ I shall crush his enemies before him,
  strike his opponents dead.

²⁴ ‘My constancy and faithful love will be with him,
  in my name his strength will be triumphant.
²⁵ I shall establish his power over the sea,
  his dominion over the rivers.

²⁶‘He will cry to me, “You are my father,
  my God, the rock of my salvation!”
²⁷ So I shall make him my first-born,
  the highest of earthly kings.

²⁸ ‘I shall maintain my faithful love for him always,
  my covenant with him will stay firm.
²⁹ I have established his dynasty for ever,

his throne to be as lasting as the heavens.

30 'Should his descendants desert my law,
   and not keep to my rulings,
31 should they violate my statutes,
   and not observe my commandments,

32 'then I shall punish their offences with the rod,
   their guilt with the whip,
33 but I shall never withdraw from him my faithful love,
   I shall not belie my constancy.

34 'I shall not violate my covenant,
I   shall not withdraw the word once spoken.
35 I have sworn by my holiness, once and for all,
   never will I break faith with David.

36 'His dynasty shall endure for ever,
   his throne like the sun before me,
37 as the moon is established for ever,
   a faithful witness in the skies.'   *Pause*

38 Yet you yourself—you have spurned and rejected,
   and have vented your wrath on your anointed,
39 you have repudiated the covenant with your servant,
   dishonoured his crown in the dust.

40 You have pierced all his defences,

and laid his strongholds in ruins,
⁴¹ everyone passing by plunders him,
he has become the butt of his neighbours.

⁴² You have raised high the right hand of his opponents,
have made all his enemies happy;
⁴³ you have snapped off his sword on a rock,
and failed to support him in battle.

⁴⁴ You have stripped him of his splendid sceptre,
and toppled his throne to the ground.
⁴⁵ You have aged him before his time,
enveloped him in shame.   *Pause*

⁴⁶ How long, Yahweh, will you remain hidden? For ever?
Is your anger to go on smouldering like a fire?
⁴⁷ Remember me; how long have I left?
For what pointless end did you create all the children
    of Adam?
⁴⁸ Who can live and never see death?
Who can save himself from the clutches of Sheol? *Pause*

⁴⁹ Lord, what of those pledges of your faithful love?
You made an oath to David by your constancy.
⁵⁰ Do not forget the insults to your servant;
I take to heart the taunts of the nations,
⁵¹ which your enemies have levelled, Yahweh,
have levelled at the footsteps of your anointed!

⁵² Blessed be Yahweh for ever.
Amen, Amen.

PSALM 90

ON HUMAN FRAILTY

Prayer   Of Moses, man of God

¹ Lord, you have been our refuge
from age to age.

² Before the mountains were born,
before the earth and the world came to birth,
from eternity to eternity you are God.

³ You bring human beings to the dust,
by saying, 'Return, children of Adam.'
⁴ A thousand years are to you
like a yesterday which has passed,
like a watch of the night.

⁵ You flood them with sleep
—in the morning they will be like growing grass:
⁶ in the morning it is blossoming and growing,
by evening it is withered and dry.

⁷ For we have been destroyed by your wrath,
dismayed by your anger.

8 You have taken note of our guilty deeds,
   our secrets in the full light of your presence.

9 All our days pass under your wrath,
   our lives are over like a sigh.
10 The span of our life is seventy years—
   eighty for those who are strong—
   but their whole extent is anxiety and trouble,
   they are over in a moment and we are gone.

11 Who feels the power of your anger,
   or who that fears you, your wrath?

12 Teach us to count up the days that are ours,
   and we shall come to the heart of wisdom.
13 Come back, Yahweh! How long must we wait?
   Take pity on your servants.

14 Each morning fill us with your faithful love,
   we shall sing and be happy all our days;
15 let our joy be as long as the time that you afflicted us,
   the years when we experienced disaster.

16 Show your servants the deeds you do,
   let their children enjoy your splendour!
17 May the sweetness of the Lord be upon us,
   to confirm the work we have done!

PSALM 91

UNDER GOD'S PROTECTION

1 You who live in the secret place of Elyon,
  spend your nights in the shelter of Shaddai,
2 saying to Yahweh, 'My refuge, my fortress,
  my God in whom I trust!'

3 He rescues you from the snare
  of the fowler set on destruction;
4 he covers you with his pinions,
  you find shelter under his wings.
  His constancy is shield and protection.

5 You need not fear the terrors of night,
  the arrow that flies in the daytime,
6 the plague that stalks in the darkness,
  the scourge that wreaks havoc at high noon.

7 Though a thousand fall at your side,
  ten thousand at your right hand,
  you yourself will remain unscathed.
8 You have only to keep your eyes open
  to see how the wicked are repaid,
9 you who say, 'Yahweh my refuge!'
  and make Elyon your fortress.

¹⁰ No disaster can overtake you,
  no plague come near your tent;
¹¹ he has given his angels orders about you
  to guard you wherever you go.

¹² They will carry you in their arms
  in case you trip over a stone.
¹³ You will walk upon wild beast and adder,
  you will trample young lions and snakes.

¹⁴ 'Since he clings to me I rescue him,
  I raise him high, since he acknowledges my name.
¹⁵ He calls to me and I answer him:
  in distress I am at his side,
  I rescue him and bring him honour.
¹⁶ I shall satisfy him with long life,
  and grant him to see my salvation.'

PSALM 92

THE SONG OF THE UPRIGHT

Psalm   Song   For the Sabbath

¹ It is good to give thanks to Yahweh,
  to make music for your name, Most High,
² to proclaim your faithful love at daybreak,
  and your constancy all through the night,
³ on the lyre, the ten-stringed lyre,

to the murmur of the harp.

4 You have brought me joy, Yahweh, by your deeds,
    at the work of your hands I cry out,
5 'How great are your works, Yahweh,
    immensely deep your thoughts!'
6 Stupid people cannot realise this,
    fools do not grasp it.

7 The wicked may sprout like weeds,
    and every evil-doer flourish,
    but only to be eternally destroyed;
8 whereas you are supreme for ever, Yahweh.

9 Look how your enemies perish,
    how all evil-doers are scattered!
10 You give me the strength of the wild ox,
you anoint me with fresh oil;
11 I caught sight of the ambush against me,
    overheard the plans of the wicked.

12 The upright will flourish like the palm tree,
    will grow like a cedar of Lebanon.
13 Planted in the house of Yahweh,
    they will flourish in the courts of our God.

14 In old age they will still bear fruit,
    will remain fresh and green,

¹⁵ to proclaim Yahweh's integrity;
my rock, in whom no fault can be found.

PSALM 93

THE MAJESTY OF GOD

¹ Yahweh is king, robed in majesty,
robed is Yahweh and girded with power.

² The world is indeed set firm, it can never be shaken;
your throne is set firm from of old,
from all eternity you exist.

³ The rivers lift up, Yahweh,
the rivers lift up their voices,
the rivers lift up their thunder.

⁴ Greater than the voice of many waters,
more majestic than the breakers of the sea,
Yahweh is majestic in the heights.

⁵ Your decrees stand firm, unshakeable,
holiness is the beauty of your house,
Yahweh, for all time to come.

PSALM 94

THE GOD OF JUSTICE

1 God of vengeance, Yahweh,
   God of vengeance, shine forth!
2 Arise, judge of the world,
   give back the proud what they deserve!

3 How long are the wicked, Yahweh,
   how long are the wicked to triumph?
4 They bluster and boast,
   they flaunt themselves, all the evil-doers.

5 They crush your people, Yahweh,
   they oppress your heritage,
6 they murder the widow and the stranger,
   bring the orphan to a violent death.

7 They say, 'Yahweh is not looking,
   the God of Jacob is taking no notice.'
8 Take notice yourselves, you coarsest of people!
   Fools, when will you learn some sense?

9 Shall he who implanted the ear not hear,
   he who fashioned the eye not see?
10 Shall he who instructs nations not punish?
   Yahweh, the teacher of all people,
11 knows human plans and how insipid they are.

¹² How blessed are those you instruct, Yahweh,
   whom you teach by means of your law,
¹³ to give them respite in evil times,
   till a pit is dug for the wicked.

¹⁴ Yahweh will not abandon his people,
   he will not desert his heritage;
¹⁵ for judgement will again become saving justice,
   and in its wake all upright hearts will follow.

¹⁶ Who rises up on my side against the wicked?
   Who stands firm on my side against all evil-doers?
¹⁷ If Yahweh did not come to my help,
   I should soon find myself dwelling in the silence.

¹⁸ I need only say, 'I am slipping,'
   for your faithful love, Yahweh, to support me;
¹⁹ however great the anxiety of my heart,
   your consolations soothe me.

²⁰ Are you partner to a destructive court,
   that gives disorder the status of law?
²¹ They make an attack on the life of the upright,
   and condemn innocent blood.

²² No! Yahweh is a stronghold to me,
   my God is my rock of refuge.
²³ He turns back their guilt on themselves,

annihilates them for their wickedness,
he annihilates them, Yahweh our God.

PSALM 95

INVITATION TO PRAISE

1 Come, let us cry out with joy to Yahweh,
  acclaim the rock of our salvation.
2 Let us come into his presence with thanksgiving,
  acclaim him with music.

3 For Yahweh is a great God,
  a king greater than all the gods.
4 In his power are the depths of the earth,
  the peaks of the mountains are his;
5 the sea belongs to him, for he made it,
  and the dry land, moulded by his hands.

6 Come, let us bow low and do reverence;
  kneel before Yahweh who made us!
7 For he is our God,
  and we the people of his sheepfold,
  the flock of his hand.

  If only you would listen to him today!
8 Do not harden your hearts as at Meribah,
  as at the time of Massah in the desert,[a]

⁹ when your ancestors challenged me,
  put me to the test, and saw what I could do!

¹⁰ For forty years that generation sickened me,
   and I said, 'Always fickle hearts;
   they cannot grasp my ways.'
¹¹ Then in my anger I swore
   they would never enter my place of rest.

PSALM 96

YAHWEH, KING AND JUDGE

¹ Sing a new song to Yahweh!
  Sing to Yahweh, all the earth!
² Sing to Yahweh, bless his name!

  Proclaim his salvation day after day,
³ declare his glory among the nations,
  his marvels to every people!

⁴ Great is Yahweh, worthy of all praise,
  more awesome than any of the gods.
⁵ All the gods of the nations are idols!

  It was Yahweh who made the heavens;
⁶ in his presence are splendour and majesty,
  in his sanctuary power and beauty.

7 Give to Yahweh, families of nations,
   give to Yahweh glory and power,
8 give to Yahweh the glory due to his name!

   Bring an offering and enter his courts,
9 adore Yahweh in the splendour of his holiness.
   Tremble before him, all the earth.

10 Say among the nations, 'Yahweh is king.'
   The world is set firm, it cannot be moved.
   He will judge the nations with justice.

11 Let the heavens rejoice and earth be glad!
   Let the sea thunder, and all it holds!
12 Let the countryside exult, and all that is in it,
   and all the trees of the forest cry out for joy,

13 at Yahweh's approach, for he is coming,
   coming to judge the earth;
   he will judge the world with saving justice,
   and the nations with constancy.

PSALM 97

THE TRIUMPH OF YAHWEH

1 Yahweh is king! Let earth rejoice,
   the many isles be glad!

² Cloud, black cloud enfolds him,
saving justice and judgement the foundations of his
throne.

³ Fire goes before him,
sets ablaze his enemies all around;
⁴ his lightning-flashes light up the world,
the earth sees it and quakes.

⁵ The mountains melt like wax,
before the Lord of all the earth.
⁶ The heavens proclaim his saving justice,
all nations see his glory.

⁷ Shame on all who serve images,
who pride themselves on their idols;
bow down to him, all you gods!

⁸ Zion hears and is glad,
the daughters of Judah exult,
because of your judgements, Yahweh.

⁹ For you are Yahweh,
Most High over all the earth,
far transcending all gods.

¹⁰ Yahweh loves those who hate evil,
he keeps safe his faithful,

rescues them from the clutches of the wicked.

[11] Light dawns for the upright,
and joy for honest hearts.
[12] Rejoice in Yahweh, you who are upright,
praise his unforgettable holiness.

PSALM 98

THE JUDGE OF THE WORLD

Psalm

[1] Sing a new song to Yahweh,
for he has performed wonders,
his saving power is in his right hand
and his holy arm.

[2] Yahweh has made known his saving power,
revealed his saving justice for the nations to see,
[3] mindful of his faithful love and his constancy
to the House of Israel.

The whole wide world has seen
the saving power of our God.
[4] Acclaim Yahweh, all the earth,
burst into shouts of joy!

[5] Play to Yahweh on the harp,

to the sound of instruments;
⁶ to the sound of trumpet and horn,
    acclaim the presence of the King.

⁷ Let the sea thunder, and all that it holds,
    the world and all who live in it.
⁸ Let the rivers clap their hands,
    and the mountains shout for joy together,

⁹ at Yahweh's approach, for he is coming
    to judge the earth;
    he will judge the world with saving justice
    and the nations with fairness.

PSALM 99

GOD, THE UPRIGHT AND HOLY KING

¹ Yahweh is king, the peoples tremble;
    he is enthroned on the winged creatures, the earth
        shivers;
² Yahweh is great in Zion.

He is supreme over all nations;
³ let them praise your name, great and awesome;
    holy is he ⁴and mighty!

You are a king who loves justice,

you established honesty, justice and uprightness;
in Jacob it is you who are active.

> [5] Exalt Yahweh our God,
>   bow down at his footstool;
>   holy is he!

[6] Moses and Aaron are among his priests, and Samuel,
calling on his name; they called on Yahweh
  and he answered them.

[7] He spoke with them in the pillar of fire,
they obeyed his decrees, the Law he gave them.

[8] Yahweh our God, you answered them,
you were a God of forgiveness to them,
  but punished them for their sins.

> [9] Exalt Yahweh our God,
>   bow down at his holy mountain;
>   holy is Yahweh our God!

PSALM 100

INVITATION TO PRAISE

Psalm   For thanksgiving

[1] Acclaim Yahweh, all the earth,

² serve Yahweh with gladness,
    come into his presence with songs of joy!

³ Be sure that Yahweh is God,
    he made us, we belong to him,
    his people, the flock of his sheepfold.

⁴ Come within his gates giving thanks,
    to his courts singing praise,
    give thanks to him and bless his name!

⁵ For Yahweh is good,
    his faithful love is everlasting,
    his constancy from age to age.

PSALM 101

THE IDEAL RULER

Of David   Psalm

¹ I will sing of faithful love and judgement;
    to you, Yahweh, will I make music.
² I will go forward in the path of the blameless;
    when will you come to me?

    I will live in purity of heart,
        in my house,

³ I will not set before my eyes
    anything sordid.

I hate those who act crookedly;
    this has no attraction for me.
⁴ Let the perverse of heart keep away from me;
    the wicked I disregard.

⁵ One who secretly slanders a comrade,
    I reduce to silence;
haughty looks, proud heart,
    these I cannot abide.

⁶ I look to the faithful of the land
    to be my companions,
only he who walks in the path of the blameless
    shall be my servant.

⁷ There is no room in my house
    for anyone who practises deceit;
no liar will stand his ground
    where I can see him.

⁸ Morning after morning I reduce to silence
    all the wicked in the land,
banishing from the city of Yahweh
    all evil-doers.

PSALM 102

PRAYER IN MISFORTUNE

Prayer of someone afflicted, who in misfortune pours out sorrows before Yahweh

1 Yahweh, hear my prayer,
   let my cry for help reach you.
2 Do not turn away your face from me
   when I am in trouble;
   bend down and listen to me,
   when I call, be quick to answer me!

3 For my days are vanishing like smoke,
   my bones burning like an oven;
4 like grass struck by blight, my heart is withering,
   I forget to eat my meals.
5 From the effort of voicing my groans
   my bones stick out through my skin.

6 I am like a desert-owl in the wastes,
   a screech-owl among ruins,
7 I keep vigil and moan
   like a lone bird on a roof.
8 All day long my enemies taunt me,
   those who once praised me now use me as a curse.

9 Ashes are the food that I eat,

my drink is mingled with tears,

[10] because of your fury and anger,
since you have raised me up only to cast me away;

[11] my days are like a fading shadow,
I am withering up like grass.

[12] But you, Yahweh, are enthroned for ever,
each generation in turn remembers you.

[13] Rise up, take pity on Zion!
the time has come to have mercy on her,
the moment has come;

[14] for your servants love her very stones,
are moved to pity by her dust.

[15] Then will the nations revere the name of Yahweh,
and all the kings of the earth your glory;

[16] when Yahweh builds Zion anew,
he will be seen in his glory;

[17] he will turn to hear the prayer of the destitute,
and will not treat their prayer with scorn.

[18] This shall be put on record for a future generation,
and a people yet to be born shall praise God:

[19] Yahweh has leaned down from the heights of his
sanctuary,
has looked down from heaven to earth,

[20] to listen to the sighing of the captive,
and set free those condemned to death,

²¹ to proclaim the name of Yahweh in Zion,
   his praise in Jerusalem;
²² nations will gather together,
   and kingdoms to worship Yahweh.

²³ In my journeying my strength has failed on the way;
²⁴ let me know the short time I have left.
   Do not take me away before half my days are done,
   for your years run on from age to age.

²⁵ Long ago you laid earth's foundations,
   the heavens are the work of your hands.
²⁶ They pass away but you remain;
   they all wear out like a garment,
   like outworn clothes you change them;
²⁷ but you never alter, and your years never end.
²⁸ The children of those who serve you will dwell secure,
   and their descendants live on in your presence.

PSALM 103

GOD IS LOVE

Of David

¹ Bless Yahweh, my soul,
   from the depths of my being, his holy name;
² bless Yahweh, my soul,
   never forget all his acts of kindness.

³ He forgives all your offences,
 cures all your diseases,
 ⁴he redeems your life from the abyss,
 crowns you with faithful love and tenderness;
⁵ he contents you with good things all your life,
 renews your youth like an eagle's.

⁶ Yahweh acts with uprightness,
 with justice to all who are oppressed;
⁷ he revealed to Moses his ways,
 his great deeds to the children of Israel.

⁸ Yahweh is tenderness and pity,
 slow to anger and rich in faithful love;
⁹ his indignation does not last for ever,
 nor his resentment remain for all time;
¹⁰ he does not treat us as our sins deserve,
 nor repay us as befits our offences.

¹¹ As the height of heaven above earth,
 so strong is his faithful love for those who fear him.
¹² As the distance of east from west,
 so far from us does he put our faults.

¹³ As tenderly as a father treats his children,
 so Yahweh treats those who fear him;
¹⁴ he knows of what we are made,
 he remembers that we are dust.

¹⁵ As for a human person—his days are like grass,
   he blooms like the wild flowers;
¹⁶ as soon as the wind blows he is gone,
   never to be seen there again.

¹⁷ But Yahweh's faithful love for those who fear him
   is from eternity and for ever;
   and his saving justice to their children's children;
¹⁸ as long as they keep his covenant,
   and carefully obey his precepts.

¹⁹ Yahweh has fixed his throne in heaven,
   his sovereign power rules over all.
²⁰ Bless Yahweh, all his angels,
   mighty warriors who fulfil his commands,
   attentive to the sound of his words.

²¹ Bless Yahweh, all his armies,
   servants who fulfil his wishes.
²² Bless Yahweh, all his works,
   in every place where he rules.

   Bless Yahweh, my soul.

PSALM 104

THE GLORIES OF CREATION

¹ Bless Yahweh, my soul,
  Yahweh, my God, how great you are!
  Clothed in majesty and splendour,
² wearing the light as a robe!

  You stretch out the heavens like a tent,
³ build your palace on the waters above,
  making the clouds your chariot,
  gliding on the wings of the wind,
⁴ appointing the winds your messengers,
  flames of fire your servants.

⁵ You fixed the earth on its foundations,
  for ever and ever it shall not be shaken;
⁶ you covered it with the deep like a garment,
  the waters overtopping the mountains.

⁷ At your reproof the waters fled,
  at the voice of your thunder they sped away,
⁸ flowing over mountains, down valleys,
  to the place you had fixed for them;
⁹ you made a limit they were not to cross,
  they were not to return and cover the earth.

¹⁰ In the ravines you opened up springs,
   running down between the mountains,
¹¹ supplying water for all the wild beasts;
   the wild asses quench their thirst,
¹² on their banks the birds of the air make their nests,
   they sing among the leaves.

¹³ From your high halls you water the mountains,
   satisfying the earth with the fruit of your works:
¹⁴ for cattle you make the grass grow,
   and for people the plants they need,
   to bring forth food from the earth,
¹⁵ and wine to cheer people's hearts,
   oil to make their faces glow,
   food to make them sturdy of heart.

¹⁶ The trees of Yahweh drink their fill,
   the cedars of Lebanon which he sowed;
¹⁷ there the birds build their nests,
   on the highest branches the stork makes its home;
¹⁸ for the wild goats there are the mountains,
   in the crags the coneys find refuge.

¹⁹ He made the moon to mark the seasons,
   the sun knows when to set.
²⁰ You bring on darkness, and night falls,
   when all the forest beasts roam around;
²¹ young lions roar for their prey,

asking God for their food.

²² The sun rises and away they steal,
back to their lairs to lie down,
²³ and man goes out to work,
to labour till evening falls.

²⁴ How countless are your works, Yahweh,
all of them made so wisely!
The earth is full of your creatures.

²⁵ Then there is the sea, with its vast expanses
teeming with countless creatures,
creatures both great and small;
²⁶ there ships pass to and fro,
and Leviathan whom you made to sport with.

²⁷ They all depend upon you,
to feed them when they need it.
²⁸ You provide the food they gather,
your open hand gives them their fill.

²⁹ Turn away your face and they panic;
take back their breath and they die
and revert to dust.
³⁰ Send out your breath and life begins;
you renew the face of the earth.

[31] Glory to Yahweh for ever!
    May Yahweh find joy in his creatures!
[32] At his glance the earth trembles,
    at his touch the mountains pour forth smoke.

[33] I shall sing to Yahweh all my life,
    make music for my God as long as I live.
[34] May my musings be pleasing to him,
    for Yahweh gives me joy.
[35] May sinners vanish from the earth,
    and the wicked exist no more!

Bless Yahweh, my soul.

PSALM 105

THE WONDERFUL HISTORY OF ISRAEL

Alleluia!

[1] Give thanks to Yahweh, call on his name,
    proclaim his deeds to the peoples!
[2] Sing to him, make music for him,
    recount all his wonders!
[3] Glory in his holy name,
    let the hearts that seek Yahweh rejoice!

[4] Seek Yahweh and his strength,

tirelessly seek his presence!

5 Remember the marvels he has done,
his wonders, the judgements he has spoken.

6 Stock of Abraham, his servant,
children of Jacob whom he chose!

7 He is Yahweh our God,
his judgements touch the whole world.

8 He remembers his covenant for ever,
the promise he laid down for a thousand generations,

9 which he concluded with Abraham,
the oath he swore to Isaac.

10 He established it as a statute for Jacob,
an everlasting covenant with Israel,

11 saying, 'To you I give a land,
Canaan, your allotted birthright.'

12 When they were insignificant in numbers,
a handful of strangers in the land,

13 wandering from country to country,
from one kingdom and nation to another,

14 he allowed no one to oppress them;
for their sake he instructed kings,

15 'Do not touch my anointed ones,
to my prophets you may do no harm.'

[16] He called down famine on the land,
he took away their food supply;
[17] he sent a man ahead of them,
Joseph, sold as a slave.

[18] So his feet were weighed down with shackles,
his neck was put in irons.
[19] In due time his prophecy was fulfilled,
the word of Yahweh proved him true.

[20] The king sent orders to release him,
the ruler of nations set him free;
[21] he put him in charge of his household,
the ruler of all he possessed,

[22] to instruct his princes as he saw fit,
to teach his counsellors wisdom.
[23] Then Israel migrated to Egypt,
Jacob settled in the country of Ham.

[24] He made his people increase in numbers,
he gave them more strength than their enemies,
[25] whose heart he turned to hate his own people,
to double-cross his servants.

[26] He sent his servant Moses,
and Aaron, the man of his choice.
[27] They worked there the wonders he commanded,

marvels in the country of Ham.

28 Darkness he sent, and darkness fell,
   but that nation defied his orders.
29 He turned their rivers to blood,
   and killed all the fish in them.

30 Their country was overrun with frogs,
   even in the royal apartments;
31 at his word came flies,
   and mosquitoes throughout the country.

32 He gave them hail as their rain,
   flames of fire in their land;
33 he blasted their vine and their fig tree,
   and shattered the trees of the country.

34 At his word came locusts,
   hoppers beyond all counting;
35 they devoured every green thing in the land,
   devoured all the produce of the soil.

36 He struck all the first-born in their land,
   the flower of all their manhood;
37 he led Israel out with silver and gold;
   in their tribes there was none who stumbled.

38 Egypt was glad at their leaving,

for terror of Israel had seized them.
[39] He spread out a cloud to cover them,
and fire to light up the night.

[40] They asked and he brought them quails,
food from heaven to their hearts' content;
[41] he opened a rock, the waters gushed out,
and flowed in dry ground as a river.

[42] Faithful to his sacred promise,
given to his servant Abraham,
[43] he led out his people with rejoicing,
his chosen ones with shouts of joy.

[44] He gave them the territories of nations,
they reaped the fruit of other people's labours,
[45] on condition that they kept his statutes,
and remained obedient to his laws.

PSALM 106

NATIONAL CONFESSION OF GUILT

[1] Alleluia!

Give thanks to Yahweh, for he is good,
his faithful love is everlasting!
[2] Who can recount all Yahweh's triumphs,

who can fully voice his praise?

3 How blessed are those who keep to what is just,
  whose conduct is always upright!
4 Remember me, Yahweh,
  in your love for your people.

  Come near to me with your saving power,
5 let me share the happiness of your chosen ones,
  let me share the joy of your people,
  the pride of your heritage.

6 Like our ancestors, we have sinned,
  we have acted wickedly, guiltily;
7 our ancestors in Egypt never grasped
  the meaning of your wonders.

  They did not bear in mind your countless acts of love,
  at the Sea of Reeds they defied the Most High;
8 but for the sake of his name he saved them,
  to make known his mighty power.

9 At his rebuke the Sea of Reeds dried up,
  he let them pass through the deep as though it were
      desert,
10 so he saved them from their opponents' clutches,
  rescued them from the clutches of their enemies.

¹¹ The waters enveloped their enemies,
   not one of whom was left.
¹² Then they believed what he had said,
   and sang his praises.

¹³ But they soon forgot his achievements,
   they did not even wait for his plans;
¹⁴ they were overwhelmed with greed in the wastelands,
   in the solitary wastes they challenged God.

¹⁵ He gave them all they asked for,
   but struck them with a deep wasting sickness;
¹⁶ in the camp they grew jealous of Moses,
   and of Aaron, Yahweh's holy one.

¹⁷ The earth opened and swallowed up Dathan,
   closed in on Abiram's faction;
¹⁸ fire flamed out against their faction,
   the renegades were engulfed in flames.

¹⁹ At Horeb they made a calf,
   bowed low before cast metal;
²⁰ they exchanged their glory
   for the image of a grass-eating bull.

²¹ They forgot the God who was saving them,
   who had done great deeds in Egypt,
²² such wonders in the land of Ham,

such awesome deeds at the Sea of Reeds.

23 He thought of putting an end to them,
had not Moses, his chosen one,
taken a stand in the breach and confronted him,
to turn his anger away from destroying them.

24 They counted a desirable land for nothing,
they put no trust in his promise;
25 they stayed in their tents and grumbled,
they would not listen to Yahweh's voice.

26 So he lifted his hand against them,
to strike them down in the desert,
27 to strike down their descendants among the nations,
to scatter them all over the world.

28 They committed themselves to serve Baal-Peor,
and ate sacrifices made to lifeless gods.
29 They so provoked him by their actions
that a plague broke out among them.

30 Then up stood Phinehas to intervene,
and the plague was checked;
31 for this he is the example of uprightness,
from age to age for ever.

32 At the waters of Meribah they so angered Yahweh,

that Moses suffered on their account,
³³ for they had embittered his spirit,
and he spoke without due thought.

³⁴ They did not destroy the nations,
as Yahweh had told them to do,
³⁵ but intermarried with them,
and adopted their ways.

³⁶ They worshipped those nations' false gods,
till they found themselves entrapped,
³⁷ and sacrificed their own sons
and their daughters to demons.

³⁸ Innocent blood they shed,
the blood of their sons and daughters;
offering them to the idols of Canaan,
they polluted the country with blood.

³⁹ They defiled themselves by such actions,
their behaviour was that of a harlot.
⁴⁰ Yahweh's anger blazed out at his people,
his own heritage filled him with disgust.

⁴¹ He handed them over to the nations,
and their opponents became their masters;
⁴² their enemies lorded it over them,
crushing them under their rule.

⁴³ Time and again he rescued them,
but they still defied him deliberately,
and sank ever deeper in their guilt;
⁴⁴ even so he took pity on their distress,
as soon as he heard them cry out.

⁴⁵ Bearing his covenant with them in mind,
he relented in his boundless and faithful love;
⁴⁶ he ensured that they received compassion,
in their treatment by all their captors.

⁴⁷ Save us, Yahweh our God,
gather us from among the nations,
that we may give thanks to your holy name,
and may glory in praising you.

⁴⁸ Blessed be Yahweh, the God of Israel,
from all eternity and for ever!
Let all the people say, 'Amen'.

PSALM 107

GOD, A REFUGE IN EVERY DANGER

Alleluia!

¹ Give thanks to Yahweh for he is good,
his faithful love lasts for ever.

² So let them say whom Yahweh redeemed,
  whom he redeemed from the power of their enemies,
³ bringing them back from foreign lands,
  from east and west, north and south.

⁴ They were wandering in the desert, in the wastelands,
  could find no way to an inhabited city;
⁵ they were hungry and thirsty,
  their life was ebbing away.

⁶ They cried out to Yahweh in their distress,
  he rescued them from their plight,
⁷ he set them on the road,
  straight to an inhabited city.

⁸ Let them thank Yahweh for his faithful love,
  for his wonders for the children of Adam!
⁹ He has fed the hungry to their hearts' content,
  filled the starving with good things.

¹⁰ Sojourners in gloom and shadow dark as death,
  fettered in misery and chains,
¹¹ for defying the orders of Yahweh,
  for scorning the plan of the Most High—
¹² he subdued their spirit by hard labour;
  if they fell there was no one to help.

¹³ They cried out to Yahweh in their distress,

he rescued them from their plight,
¹⁴ he brought them out from gloom and shadow dark as
    death,
  and shattered their chains.

¹⁵ Let them thank Yahweh for his faithful love,
  for his wonders for the children of Adam!
¹⁶ He broke open gates of bronze
  and smashed iron bars.

¹⁷ Fools for their rebellious ways,
  wretched because of their sins,
¹⁸ finding all food repugnant,
  brought close to the gates of death—

¹⁹ they cried out to Yahweh in their distress;
  he rescued them from their plight,
²⁰ he sent out his word and cured them,
  and rescued their life from the abyss.

²¹ Let them thank Yahweh for his faithful love,
  for his wonders for the children of Adam!
²² Let them offer thanksgiving sacrifices,
  and recount with shouts of joy what he has done!

²³ Voyagers on the sea in ships,
  plying their trade on the great ocean,
²⁴ have seen the works of Yahweh,

his wonders in the deep.

25 By his word he raised a storm-wind,
   lashing up towering waves.
26 Up to the sky then down to the depths!
   Their stomachs were turned to water;
27 they staggered and reeled like drunkards,
   and all their skill went under.

28 They cried out to Yahweh in their distress,
   he rescued them from their plight,
29 he reduced the storm to a calm,
   and all the waters subsided,
30 and he brought them, overjoyed at the stillness,
   to the port where they were bound.

31 Let them thank Yahweh for his faithful love,
   for his wonders for the children of Adam!
32 Let them extol him in the assembly of the people,
   and praise him in the council of elders.

33 He has turned rivers into desert,
   bubbling springs into arid ground,
34 fertile country into salt-flats,
   because the people living there were evil.

35 But he has turned desert into stretches of water,
   arid ground into bubbling springs,

³⁶ and has given the hungry a home,
    where they have built themselves a city.

³⁷ There they sow fields and plant vines,
    and reap a harvest of their produce.
³⁸ He blesses them and their numbers increase,
    he keeps their cattle at full strength.

³⁹ Their numbers had fallen, they had grown weak,
    under pressure of disaster and hardship;
⁴⁰ he covered princes in contempt,
    left them to wander in trackless wastes.

⁴¹ But the needy he raises from their misery,
    makes their families as numerous as sheep.
⁴² At the sight the honest rejoice,
    and the wicked have nothing to say.

⁴³ Who is wise? Such a one should take this to heart,
    and come to understand Yahweh's faithful love.

PSALM 108

MORNING HYMN AND NATIONAL PRAYER

Song   Psalm   Of David

¹ My heart is ready, God,

    I will sing and make music;
      come, my glory!
2 Awake, lyre and harp,
    I will awake the Dawn!

3 I will praise you among the peoples, Yahweh,
    I will play to you among nations,
4 for your faithful love towers to heaven,
    and your constancy to the clouds.

5 Be exalted above the heavens, God.
    Your glory over the whole earth!

6 To rescue those you love,
    save with your right hand and answer us.

7 God has spoken from his sanctuary,
' In triumph I will divide up Shechem,
    and share out the Valley of Succoth.

8 'Mine is Gilead, mine Manasseh,
    Ephraim the helmet on my head,
    Judah my commander's baton,

9' Moab a bowl for me to wash in,
    on Edom I plant my sandal,
    over Philistia I cry victory.'

¹⁰ Who will lead me against a fortified city,
who will guide me into Edom,
¹¹ if not you, the God who has rejected us?
God, you no longer march with our armies.

¹² Bring us help in our time of crisis,
any human assistance is worthless.
¹³ With God we shall do deeds of valour,
he will trample down our enemies.

PSALM 109

AN IMPRECATION

For the choirmaster   Of David   Psalm

¹ God whom I praise, do not be silent!
² Wicked and deceiving words
are being said about me,
false accusations are cast in my teeth.
³ Words of hate fly all around me,
though I give no cause for hostility.

⁴ In return for my friendship they denounce me,
and all I can do is pray!
⁵ They repay my kindness with evil,
and friendship with hatred.

⁶‘ Set up a wicked man against him
    as accuser to stand on his right.
⁷ At his trial may he emerge as guilty,
    even his prayer construed as a crime!

⁸ ‘May his life be cut short,
    someone else take over his office,
⁹ his children be orphaned,
    his wife be widowed.

¹⁰ ‘May his children wander perpetually,
    beggars, driven from the ruins of their house,
¹¹ a creditor seize all his goods,
    and strangers make off with his earnings.

¹² ‘May there be none left faithful enough to show him
    love,
    no one take pity on his orphans,
¹³ the line of his descendants cut off,
    his name wiped out in one generation.

¹⁴ ‘May Yahweh never forget the crimes of his ancestors,
    and his mother’s sins not be wiped out;
¹⁵ may Yahweh keep these constantly in mind,
    to cut off the remembrance of them from the earth.’

¹⁶ He had no thought of being loyal,

but hounded the poor and the needy
and the broken-hearted to their death.

¹⁷ He had a taste for cursing; let it recoil on him!
No taste for blessing; let it never come his way!

¹⁸ Cursing has been the uniform he wore;
let it soak into him like water,
like oil right into his bones.

¹⁹ Let it be as a robe which envelops him completely,
a sash which he always wears.

²⁰ Let this be the salary Yahweh pays
the accusers who blacken my name.

²¹ Yahweh, treat them as your name demands;
as your faithful love is generous, deliver me.

²² Poor and needy as I am,
my wounds go right to the heart;

²³ I am passing away like a fading shadow,
they have shaken me off like a locust.

²⁴ My knees are weak from lack of food,
my body lean for lack of fat.

²⁵ I have become the butt of their taunts,
they shake their heads at the sight of me.

²⁶ Help me, Yahweh my God,
save me as your faithful love demands.

^{27} Let them know that yours is the saving hand,
  that this, Yahweh, is your work.

^{28} Let them curse, provided that you bless;
  let their attacks bring shame to them and joy to your
    servant!
^{29} Let my accusers be clothed in disgrace,
  enveloped in a cloak of shame.

^{30} With generous thanks to Yahweh on my lips,
  I shall praise him before all the people,
^{31} for he stands at the side of the poor,
  to save their lives from those who sit in judgement on
    them.

PSALM 110

THE PRIEST MESSIAH

Of David   Psalm

^{1} Yahweh declared to my Lord, 'Take your seat at my
    right hand,
  till I have made your enemies your footstool.'

^{2} Yahweh will stretch out the sceptre of your power;
  from Zion you will rule your foes all around you.
^{3} Royal[a] dignity has been yours from the day of your
    birth,

sacred honour from the womb, from the dawn of your
  youth.

⁴ Yahweh has sworn an oath he will never retract,
  you are a priest for ever of the order of Melchizedek.

⁵ At your right hand, Lord,
  he shatters kings when his anger breaks out.
⁶ He judges nations, heaping up corpses,
  he breaks heads over the whole wide world.
⁷ He drinks from a stream as he goes,
  and therefore he holds his head high.

PSALM 111

IN PRAISE OF YAHWEH'S DEEDS

¹ Alleluia!

Aleph	I give thanks to Yahweh with all my heart,
Bet	in the meeting-place of honest people, in the assembly.
Gimel	² Great are the deeds of Yahweh,
Dalet	to be pondered by all who delight in them.
He	³ Full of splendour and majesty his work,
Waw	his saving justice stands firm for ever.
Zain	⁴ He gives us a memorial of his great deeds;

Het	Yahweh is mercy and tenderness.

Tet	5 He gives food to those who fear him,
Yod	he keeps his covenant ever in mind.
Kaph	6 His works show his people his power
Lamed	in giving them the birthright of the nations.

Mem	7 The works of his hands are fidelity and justice,
Nun	all his precepts are trustworthy,
Samek	8 established for ever and ever,
Ain	accomplished in fidelity and honesty.

Pe	9 Deliverance he sends to his people,
Zade	his covenant he imposes for ever;
Qoph	holy and awesome his name.
Resh	10 The root of wisdom is fear of Yahweh;
Shin	those who attain it are wise.
Taw	His praise will continue for ever.

PSALM 112

PRAISE OF THE UPRIGHT

1 Alleluia!

Aleph	How blessed is anyone who fears Yahweh,
Bet	who delights in his commandments!
Gimel	2 His descendants shall be powerful on earth,

Dalet   the race of the honest shall receive blessings:

He   3 Riches and wealth for his family;
Waw   his uprightness stands firm for ever.
Zain   4 For the honest he shines as a lamp in the dark,
Het   generous, tender-hearted, and upright.

Tet   5 All goes well for one who lends generously,
Yod   who is honest in all his dealing;
Kaph   6 for all time to come he will not stumble,
Lamed   for all time to come the upright will be
              remembered.

Mem   7 Bad news holds no fears for him,
Nun   firm is his heart, trusting in Yahweh.
Samek   8 His heart held steady, he has no fears,
Ain   till he can gloat over his enemies.

Pe   9 To the needy he gives without stint,
Zade   his uprightness stands firm for ever;
Qoph   his reputation is founded on strength.

Resh   10 The wicked are vexed at the sight,
Shin   they grind their teeth and waste away.
Taw   The desires of the wicked will be frustrated.

PSALM 113

TO THE GOD OF GLORY AND MERCY

[1] Alleluia!

Praise, servants of Yahweh,
praise the name of Yahweh.
[2] Blessed be the name of Yahweh,
henceforth and for ever.
[3] From the rising of the sun to its setting,
praised be the name of Yahweh!

[4] Supreme over all nations is Yahweh,
supreme over the heavens his glory.
[5] Who is like Yahweh our God?
His throne is set on high,
[6] but he stoops to look down on heaven and earth.

[7] He raises the poor from the dust,
he lifts the needy from the dunghill,
[8] to give them a place among princes,
among princes of his people.
[9] He lets the barren woman be seated at home,
the happy mother of sons.

PSALM 114

PASSOVER HYMN

Alleluia!

1 When Israel came out of Egypt,
  the House of Jacob from a people of foreign speech,
2 Judah became his sanctuary,
  and Israel his domain.

3 The sea fled at the sight,
  the Jordan turned back,
4 the mountains skipped like rams,
  the hills like sheep.

5 Sea, what makes you flee?
  Jordan, why turn back?
6 Why skip like rams, you mountains?
  Why like sheep, you hills?

7 Tremble, earth, at the coming of the Lord,
  at the coming of the God of Jacob,
8 who turns rock into pool,
  flint into fountain.

PSALM 115

THE ONE TRUE GOD

¹ Not to us, Yahweh, not to us,
  but to your name give the glory,
  for your faithful love and your constancy!
² Why should the nations ask, 'Where is their God?'

³ Our God is in heaven,
  he creates whatever he chooses.
⁴ They have idols of silver and gold,
  made by human hands.

⁵ These have mouths but say nothing,
  have eyes but see nothing,
⁶ have ears but hear nothing,
  have noses but smell nothing.

⁷ They have hands but cannot feel,
  have feet but cannot walk,
  no sound comes from their throats.
⁸ Their makers will end up like them,
  and all who rely on them.

⁹ House of Israel, rely on Yahweh;
  he is their help and their shield.
¹⁰ House of Aaron, rely on Yahweh;
  he is their help and their shield.

¹¹ You who fear Yahweh, rely on Yahweh;
  he is their help and their shield.

¹² Yahweh will keep us in mind, he will bless,
  he will bless the House of Israel,
  he will bless the House of Aaron,
¹³ he will bless those who fear Yahweh,
  small and great alike.

¹⁴ May Yahweh add to your numbers,
  yours and your children's too!
¹⁵ May you be blessed by Yahweh,
  who made heaven and earth.

¹⁶ Heaven belongs to Yahweh,
  but earth he has given to the children of Adam.

¹⁷ The dead cannot praise Yahweh,
  those who sink into silence,
¹⁸ but we, the living, shall bless Yahweh,
  henceforth and for ever.

PSALM 116

THANKSGIVING

Alleluia!

1 I am filled with love when Yahweh listens
     to the sound of my prayer,
2 when he bends down to hear me,
   as I call.

3 The bonds of death were all round me,
     the snares of Sheol held me fast;
   distress and anguish held me in their grip,
       4 I called on the name of Yahweh.

   Deliver me, Yahweh, I beg you.

5 Yahweh is merciful and upright,
     our God is tenderness.
6 Yahweh looks after the simple,
     when I was brought low he gave me strength.

7 My heart, be at peace once again,
     for Yahweh has treated you generously.
8 He has rescued me from death, my eyes from tears,
     and my feet from stumbling.
9 I shall pass my life in the presence of Yahweh,
     in the land of the living.

¹⁰ My trust does not fail even when I say,
    'I am completely wretched.'
¹¹ In my terror I said,
    'No human being can be relied on.'
¹² What return can I make to Yahweh
    for his generosity to me?
¹³ I shall take up the cup of salvation
    and call on the name of Yahweh.

¹⁴ I shall fulfil my vows to Yahweh,
    witnessed by all his people.

¹⁵ Costly in Yahweh's sight
    is the death of his faithful.

¹⁶ I beg you, Yahweh! I am your servant,
  I am your servant and my mother was your servant;
    you have undone my fetters.
¹⁷ I shall offer you a sacrifice of thanksgiving
    and call on the name of Yahweh.

¹⁸ I shall fulfil my vows to Yahweh,
    witnessed by all his people,
¹⁹ in the courts of the house of Yahweh,
    in your very heart, Jerusalem.

PSALM 117

SUMMONS TO PRAISE

Alleluia!

1 Praise Yahweh, all nations,
   extol him, all peoples,
2 for his faithful love is strong
   and his constancy never-ending.

PSALM 118

PROCESSIONAL HYMN FOR THE FEAST OF SHELTERS

Alleluia!

1 Give thanks to Yahweh for he is good,
   for his faithful love endures for ever.

2 Let the House of Israel say,
   'His faithful love endures for ever.'
3 Let the House of Aaron say,
   'His faithful love endures for ever.'
4 Let those who fear Yahweh say,
   'His faithful love endures for ever.'

5 In my distress I called to Yahweh,

he heard me and brought me relief.

6 With Yahweh on my side I fear nothing;
 what can human beings do to me?
7 With Yahweh on my side as my help,
 I gloat over my enemies.

8 It is better to take refuge in Yahweh
 than to rely on human beings;
9 better to take refuge in Yahweh
 than to rely on princes.

10 Nations were swarming around me,
 in the name of Yahweh I cut them down;
11 they swarmed around me, pressing upon me,
 in the name of Yahweh I cut them down.
12 They swarmed around me like bees,
 they flared up like a brushwood fire,
 in the name of Yahweh I cut them down.

13 I was pushed hard, to make me fall,
 but Yahweh came to my help.
14 Yahweh is my strength and my song,
 he has been my Saviour.

15 Shouts of joy and salvation,
 in the tents of the upright,
' Yahweh's right hand is triumphant,
16 Yahweh's right hand is victorious,

Yahweh's right hand is triumphant!'

¹⁷ I shall not die, I shall live
  to recount the great deeds of Yahweh.
¹⁸ Though Yahweh punished me sternly,
  he has not abandoned me to death.

¹⁹ Open for me the gates of saving justice,
  I shall go in and thank Yahweh.
²⁰ This is the gate of Yahweh,
  where the upright go in.
²¹ I thank you for hearing me,
  and making yourself my Saviour.

²² The stone which the builders rejected
  has become the cornerstone;
²³ This is Yahweh's doing,
  and we marvel at it.
²⁴ This is the day which Yahweh has made,
  a day for us to rejoice and be glad.

²⁵ We beg you, Yahweh, save us,
  we beg you, Yahweh, give us victory!
²⁶ Blessed in the name of Yahweh is he who is coming!
  We bless you from the house of Yahweh.
²⁷ Yahweh is God,
  he gives us light.

Link your processions, branches in hand,
up to the horns of the altar.

28 You are my God, I thank you,
   all praise to you, my God.
I thank you for hearing me,
   and making yourself my Saviour.

29 Give thanks to Yahweh for he is good,
for his faithful love endures for ever.

PSALM 119

IN PRAISE OF THE DIVINE LAW

Aleph 1 How blessed are those whose way is blameless,
            who walk in the Law of Yahweh!
         2 Blessed are those who observe his instructions,
            who seek him with all their hearts,
         3 and, doing no evil,
            who walk in his ways.
         4 You lay down your precepts
            to be carefully kept.
         5 May my ways be steady
            in doing your will.
         6 Then I shall not be shamed,
            if my gaze is fixed on your commandments.
         7 I thank you with a sincere heart
            for teaching me your upright judgements.

8 I shall do your will;
do not ever abandon me wholly.

Bet 9 How can a young man keep his way spotless?
By keeping your words.

10 With all my heart I seek you,
do not let me stray from your commandments.

11 In my heart I treasure your promises,
to avoid sinning against you.

12 Blessed are you, Yahweh,
teach me your will!

13 With my lips I have repeated
all the judgements you have given.

14 In the way of your instructions lies my joy,
a joy beyond all wealth.

15 I will ponder your precepts
and fix my gaze on your paths.

16 I find my delight in your will,
I do not forget your words.

Gimel 17 Be generous to your servant and I shall live,
and shall keep your words.

18 Open my eyes and I shall fix my gaze
on the wonders of your Law.

19 Wayfarer though I am on the earth,
do not hide your commandments from me.

20 My heart is pining away with longing
at all times for your judgements.

²¹ You have rebuked the arrogant, the accursed,
who stray from your commandments.

²² Set me free from taunts and contempt
since I observe your instructions.

²³ Though princes sit plotting against me,
your servant keeps pondering your will.

²⁴ Your instructions are my delight,
your wishes my counsellors.

Dalet ²⁵ Down in the dust I lie prostrate;
true to your word, revive me.

²⁶ I tell you my ways and you answer me;
teach me your wishes.

²⁷ Show me the way of your precepts,
that I may reflect on your wonders.

²⁸ I am melting away for grief;
true to your word, raise me up.

²⁹ Keep me far from the way of deceit,
grant me the grace of your Law.

³⁰ I have chosen the way of constancy,
I have moulded myself to your judgements.

³¹ I cling to your instructions,
Yahweh, do not disappoint me.

³² I run the way of your commandments,
for you have given me freedom of heart.

He ³³ Teach me, Yahweh, the way of your will,
and I will observe it.

³⁴ Give me understanding and I will observe
        your Law,
    and keep it wholeheartedly.
³⁵ Guide me in the way of your commandments,
    for my delight is there.
³⁶ Bend my heart to your instructions,
    not to selfish gain.
³⁷ Avert my eyes from pointless images,
    by your word give me life.
³⁸ Keep your promise to your servant
    so that all may hold you in awe.
³⁹ Avert the taunts that I dread,
    for your judgements are generous.
⁴⁰ See how I yearn for your precepts;
    in your saving justice give me life.

Waw ⁴¹ Let your faithful love come to me, Yahweh,
    true to your promise, save me!
⁴² Give me an answer to the taunts against me,
    since I rely on your word.
⁴³ Do not deprive me of that faithful word,
    since my hope lies in your judgements.
⁴⁴ I shall keep your Law without fail
    for ever and ever.
⁴⁵ I shall live in all freedom
    because I have sought your precepts.
⁴⁶ I shall speak of your instructions before kings
    and will not be shamed.

⁴⁷ Your commandments fill me with delight,
I love them dearly.
⁴⁸ I stretch out my hands to your commandments
that I love,
and I ponder your judgements.

Zain   ⁴⁹ Keep in mind your promise to your servant
on which I have built my hope.
⁵⁰ It is my comfort in distress,
that your promise gives me life.
⁵¹ Endlessly the arrogant have jeered at me,
but I have not swerved from your Law.
⁵² I have kept your age-old judgements in mind,
Yahweh, and I am comforted.
⁵³ Fury grips me when I see the wicked
who abandon your Law.
⁵⁴ Your judgements are my song
where I live in exile.
⁵⁵ All night, Yahweh, I hold your name in mind,
I keep your Law.
⁵⁶ This is what it means to me,
observing your precepts.

Het   ⁵⁷ My task, I have said, Yahweh,
is to keep your word.
⁵⁸ Wholeheartedly I entreat your favour;
true to your promise, take pity on me!
⁵⁹ I have reflected on my ways,

and I turn my steps to your instructions.

⁶⁰ I hurry without delay
to keep your commandments.

⁶¹ Though caught in the snares of the wicked,
I do not forget your Law.

⁶² At midnight I rise to praise you
for your upright judgements.

⁶³ I am a friend to all who fear you
and keep your precepts.

⁶⁴ Your faithful love fills the earth,
Yahweh, teach me your judgements.

Tet　⁶⁵ You have been generous to your servant,
　　　　Yahweh,
true to your promise.

⁶⁶ Teach me judgement and knowledge,
for I rely on your commandments.

⁶⁷ Before I was punished I used to go astray,
but now I keep to your promise.

⁶⁸ You are generous and act generously,
teach me your will.

⁶⁹ The arrogant blacken me with lies
though I wholeheartedly observe your precepts.

⁷⁰ Their hearts are gross like rich fat,
but my delight is in your Law.

⁷¹ It was good for me that I had to suffer,
the better to learn your judgements.

⁷² The Law you have uttered is more precious to me

than all the wealth in the world.

Yod   ⁷³ Your hands have made me and held me firm,
give me understanding and I shall learn your
    commandments.
⁷⁴ Those who fear you rejoice at the sight of me
since I put my hope in your word.
⁷⁵ I know, Yahweh, that your judgements are
    upright,
and in punishing me you show your constancy.
⁷⁶ Your faithful love must be my consolation,
as you have promised your servant.
⁷⁷ Treat me with tenderness and I shall live,
for your Law is my delight.
⁷⁸ Let the arrogant who tell lies against me be
    shamed,
while I ponder your precepts.
⁷⁹ Let those who fear you rally to me,
those who understand your instructions.
⁸⁰ My heart shall be faultless towards your will;
then I shall not be ashamed.

Kaph   ⁸¹ I shall wear myself out for your salvation,
for your word is my hope.
⁸² My eyes, too, are worn out waiting for your
    promise,
when will you have pity on me?
⁸³ For I am like a smoked wineskin,

but I do not forget your will.

84 How long has your servant to live?
When will you bring my persecutors to
judgement?

85 The arrogant have dug pitfalls for me
in defiance of your Law.

86 All your commandments show constancy.
Help me when they pursue me dishonestly.

87 They have almost annihilated me on earth,
but I have not deserted your precepts.

88 True to your faithful love, give me life,
and I shall keep the instructions you have laid
down.

Lamed 89 For ever, Yahweh, your word
is planted firm in heaven.

90 Your constancy endures from age to age;
you established the earth and it stands firm.

91 Through your judgements all stands firm to
this day,
for all creation is your servant.

92 Had your Law not been my delight,
I would have perished in my misery.

93 I shall never forget your precepts,
for by them you have given me life.

94 I am yours, save me,
for I seek your precepts.

95 The wicked may hope to destroy me,

but all my thought is of your instructions.

⁹⁶ I have seen that all perfection is finite,
but your commandment has no limit.

Mem ⁹⁷ How I love your Law!
I ponder it all day long.

⁹⁸ You make me wiser than my enemies
by your commandment which is mine for ever.

⁹⁹ I am wiser than all my teachers
because I ponder your instructions.

¹⁰⁰ I have more understanding than the aged
because I keep your precepts.

¹⁰¹ I restrain my foot from evil paths
to keep your word.

¹⁰² I do not turn aside from your judgements,
because you yourself have instructed me.

¹⁰³ How pleasant your promise to my palate,
sweeter than honey in my mouth!

¹⁰⁴ From your precepts I learn wisdom,
so I hate all deceptive ways.

Nun ¹⁰⁵ Your word is a lamp for my feet,
a light on my path.

¹⁰⁶ I have sworn—and shall maintain it—
to keep your upright judgements.

¹⁰⁷ I am utterly wretched, Yahweh;
true to your promise, give me life.

¹⁰⁸ Accept, Yahweh, the tribute from my mouth,

and teach me your judgements.

[109] My life is in your hands perpetually,
I do not forget your Law.

[110] The wicked have laid out a snare for me,
but I have not strayed from your precepts.

[111] Your instructions are my eternal heritage,
they are the joy of my heart.

[112] I devote myself to obeying your statutes,
their recompense is eternal.

Samek [113] I hate a divided heart,
I love your Law.

[114] You are my refuge and shield,
I put my hope in your word.

[115] Leave me alone, you wicked,
I shall observe the commandments of my God.

[116] True to your word, support me and I shall live;
do not disappoint me of my hope.

[117] Uphold me and I shall be saved,
my gaze fixed on your will.

[118] You shake off all who stray from your will;
deceit fills their horizon.

[119] In your sight all the wicked of the earth are
like rust,
so I love your instructions.

[120] My whole body trembles before you,
your judgements fill me with fear.

Ain   ¹²¹ All my conduct has been just and upright,
do not hand me over to my oppressors.

¹²² Guarantee the well-being of your servant,
do not let the proud oppress me.

¹²³ My eyes are languishing for your salvation
and for the saving justice you have promised.

¹²⁴ Show your faithful love to your servant,
teach me your judgements.

¹²⁵ Your servant am I; give me understanding
and I shall know your instructions.

¹²⁶ It is time to take action, Yahweh,
your Law is being broken.

¹²⁷ So I love your commandments
more than gold, purest gold.

¹²⁸ So I rule my life by your precepts,
I hate all deceptive paths.

Pe   ¹²⁹ Wonderful are your instructions,
so I observe them.

¹³⁰ As your word unfolds it gives light,
and even the simple understand.

¹³¹ I open wide my mouth,
panting eagerly for your commandments.

¹³² Turn to me, pity me;
those who love your name deserve it.

¹³³ Keep my steps firm in your promise;
that no evil may triumph over me.

¹³⁴ Rescue me from human oppression,

and I will observe your precepts.

¹³⁵ Let your face shine on your servant,
teach me your will.

¹³⁶ My eyes stream with tears
because your Law is disregarded.

Zade ¹³⁷ You are upright, Yahweh,
and your judgements are honest.

¹³⁸ You impose uprightness as a witness to
yourself,
it is constancy itself.

¹³⁹ My zeal is burning me up
because my oppressors forget your word.

¹⁴⁰ Your promise is well tested,
your servant holds it dear.

¹⁴¹ Puny and despised as I am,
I do not forget your precepts.

¹⁴² Your saving justice is for ever just,
and your Law is trustworthy.

¹⁴³ Though anguish and distress grip me
your commandments are my delight.

¹⁴⁴ Your instructions are upright for ever,
give me understanding and I shall live.

Qoph ¹⁴⁵ I call with all my heart; answer me, Yahweh,
and I will observe your judgements.

¹⁴⁶ I call to you; save me,
and I will keep your instructions.

¹⁴⁷ I am awake before dawn to cry for help,
   I put my hope in your word.
¹⁴⁸ My eyes are awake before each watch of the
      night,
   to ponder your promise.
¹⁴⁹ In your faithful love, Yahweh, listen to my
      voice,
   let your judgements give me life.
¹⁵⁰ My pursuers are coming closer to their
      wicked designs,
   and further from your Law.
¹⁵¹ You are close to me, Yahweh,
   and all your commandments are true.
¹⁵² Long have I known that your instructions
   were laid down to last for ever.

Resh ¹⁵³ Look at my suffering and rescue me,
   for I do not forget your Law.
¹⁵⁴ Plead my cause and defend me;
   as you promised, give me life.
¹⁵⁵ Salvation is far from the wicked,
   for they do not seek your will.
¹⁵⁶ Your kindnesses to me are countless, Yahweh;
   true to your judgements, give me life.
¹⁵⁷ Though my enemies and oppressors are
      countless,
   I do not turn aside from your instructions.
¹⁵⁸ The sight of these renegades appals me;

they do not observe your promise.

¹⁵⁹ See how I love your precepts;
true to your faithful love, give me life.

¹⁶⁰ Faithfulness is the essence of your word,
your upright judgements hold good for ever.

Shin   ¹⁶¹ Though princes hound me unprovoked,
what fills me with awe is your word.

¹⁶² I rejoice in your promise
like one who finds a vast treasure.

¹⁶³ Falsehood I hate and detest,
my love is for your Law.

¹⁶⁴ Seven times a day I praise you
for your upright judgements.

¹⁶⁵ Great peace for those who love your Law;
no stumbling-blocks for them!

¹⁶⁶ I am waiting for your salvation, Yahweh,
I fulfil your commandments.

¹⁶⁷ I observe your instructions,
I love them dearly.

¹⁶⁸ I observe your precepts, your judgements,
for all my ways are before you.

Taw   ¹⁶⁹ May my cry approach your presence, Yahweh;
by your word give me understanding.

¹⁷⁰ May my prayer come into your presence,
rescue me as you have promised.

¹⁷¹ May my lips proclaim your praise,

for you teach me your will.

¹⁷² May my tongue recite your promise,
for all your commandments are upright.

¹⁷³ May your hand be there to help me,
since I have chosen your precepts.

¹⁷⁴ I long for your salvation, Yahweh,
your Law is my delight.

¹⁷⁵ May I live only to praise you,
may your judgements be my help.

¹⁷⁶ I am wandering like a lost sheep,
come and look for your servant,
for I have not forgotten your commandments.

PSALM 120

THE ENEMIES OF PEACE

Song of Ascentsa

¹ To Yahweh when I am in trouble
I call and he answers me.

² Yahweh, save me from lying lips
and a treacherous tongue!

³ What will he repay you, what more,
treacherous tongue?

⁴ War-arrows made sharp
over red-hot charcoal.

5 How wretched I am, living in Meshech,
   dwelling in the tents of Kedar!

6 Too long have I lived
   among people who hate peace.
7 When I speak of peace
   they are all for war!

PSALM 121

THE GUARDIAN OF ISRAEL

Song of Ascents

1 I lift up my eyes to the mountains;
   where is my help to come from?
2 My help comes from Yahweh
   who made heaven and earth.

3 May he save your foot from stumbling;
   may he, your guardian, not fall asleep!
4 You see—he neither sleeps nor slumbers,
   the guardian of Israel.

5 Yahweh is your guardian, your shade,
   Yahweh, at your right hand.
6 By day the sun will not strike you,
   nor the moon by night.

7 Yahweh guards you from all harm
   Yahweh guards your life,
8 Yahweh guards your comings and goings,
   henceforth and for ever.

PSALM 122

HAIL, JERUSALEM

Song of Ascents   Of David

1 I rejoiced that they said to me,
   'Let us go to the house of Yahweh.'
2 At last our feet are standing
   at your gates, Jerusalem!

3 Jerusalem, built as a city,
   in one united whole,
4 there the tribes go up,
   the tribes of Yahweh,
 a sign for Israel to give thanks
   to the name of Yahweh.
5 For there are set the thrones of judgement,
   the thrones of the house of David.

6 Pray for the peace of Jerusalem,
   prosperity for your homes!
7 Peace within your walls,
   prosperity in your palaces!

8 For love of my brothers and my friends
   I will say, 'Peace upon you!'
9 For love of the house of Yahweh our God
   I will pray for your well-being.

PSALM 123

PRAYER IN DISTRESS

Song of Ascents

1 I lift up my eyes to you
   who are enthroned in heaven.
2 Just as the eyes of slaves
   are on their masters' hand,

or the eyes of a slave-girl
   on the hand of her mistress,
so our eyes are on Yahweh our God,
   for him to take pity on us.

3 Have pity on us, Yahweh, have pity,
   for we have had our full share of scorn,
4 more than our share
   of jeers from the complacent.

(Scorn is for the proud.)

PSALM 124

THE SAVIOUR OF ISRAEL

Song of Ascents   Of David

¹ If Yahweh had not been on our side
    —let Israel repeat it—
² if Yahweh had not been on our side
    when people attacked us,
³ they would have swallowed us alive
    in the heat of their anger.

⁴ Then water was washing us away,
    a torrent running right over us;
⁵ running right over us then
    were turbulent waters.

⁶ Blessed be Yahweh for not letting us fall
    a prey to their teeth!
⁷ We escaped like a bird
    from the fowlers' net.

The net was broken
    and we escaped;
⁸ our help is in the name of Yahweh,
    who made heaven and earth.

PSALM 125

GOD PROTECTS HIS FAITHFUL

Song of Ascents

1 Whoever trusts in Yahweh is like Mount Zion:
    unshakeable, it stands for ever.
2 Jerusalem! The mountains encircle her:
so Yahweh encircles his people,
    henceforth and for ever.

3 The sceptre of the wicked will not come to rest
    over the heritage of the upright;
or the upright might set
    their own hands to evil.

4 Do good, Yahweh, to those who are good,
    to the sincere at heart.
5 But the crooked, the twisted, turn them away,
    Yahweh, with evil-doers.

Peace to Israel!

PSALM 126

SONG OF THE RETURNING EXILES

Song of Ascents

1 When Yahweh brought back Zion's captives
   we lived in a dream;
2 then our mouths filled with laughter,
   and our lips with song.

   Then the nations kept saying, 'What great deeds
      Yahweh has done for them!'
3 Yes, Yahweh did great deeds for us,
   and we were overjoyed.

4 Bring back, Yahweh, our people from captivity
   like torrents in the Negeb!
5 Those who sow in tears
   sing as they reap.

6 He went off, went off weeping,
   carrying the seed.
   He comes back, comes back singing,
      bringing in his sheaves.

PSALM 127

TRUST IN PROVIDENCE

Song of Ascents   Of Solomon

1   If Yahweh does not build a house
    in vain do its builders toil.
    If Yahweh does not guard a city
    in vain does its guard keep watch.

2   In vain you get up earlier,
    and put off going to bed,
    sweating to make a living,
    since it is he who provides for his beloved as they sleep.

3   Sons are a birthright from Yahweh,
    children are a reward from him.
4   Like arrows in a warrior's hand
    are the sons you father when young.

5   How blessed is the man
    who has filled his quiver with them;
    in dispute with his enemies at the city gate
    he will not be worsted.

PSALM 128

BLESSING ON THE FAITHFUL

Song of Ascents

¹ How blessed are all who fear Yahweh,
    who walk in his ways!

² Your own labours will yield you a living,
    happy and prosperous will you be.
³ Your wife a fruitful vine
    in the inner places of your house.
  Your children round your table
    like shoots of an olive tree.

⁴ Such are the blessings that fall
    on those who fear Yahweh.
⁵ May Yahweh bless you from Zion!
    May you see Jerusalem prosper
    all the days of your life,
⁶ and live to see your children's children!

Peace to Israel!

PSALM 129

AGAINST ZION'S ENEMIES

Song of Ascents

1 Often as men have attacked me since I was young
    —let Israel repeat it—
2 often as men have attacked me since I was young,
    they have never overcome me.

3 On my back ploughmen have set to work,
    making long furrows,
4 but Yahweh the upright has shattered
    the yoke of the wicked.

5 Let all who hate Zion
    be thrown back in confusion,
6 let them be like grass on a roof,
    dried up before it is cut,
7 never to fill the reaper's arm
    nor the binder's lap.
8 And no passer-by will say,
    'The blessing of Yahweh be on you!

'We bless you in the name of Yahweh.'

PSALM 130

OUT OF THE DEPTHS

Song of Ascents

¹ From the depths I call to you, Yahweh:
    ² Lord, hear my cry.
  Listen attentively
      to the sound of my pleading!

³ If you kept a record of our sins,
      Lord, who could stand their ground?
⁴ But with you is forgiveness,
      that you may be revered.

⁵ I rely, my whole being relies,
      Yahweh, on your promise.
⁶ My whole being hopes in the Lord,
      more than watchmen for daybreak;
  more than watchmen for daybreak
      ⁷ let Israel hope in Yahweh.

  For with Yahweh is faithful love,
      with him generous ransom;
⁸ and he will ransom Israel
      from all its sins.

PSALM 131

CHILDLIKE TRUST

Song of Ascents

1 Yahweh, my heart is not haughty,
    I do not set my sights too high.
  I have taken no part in great affairs,
    in wonders beyond my scope.
2 No, I hold myself in quiet and silence,
    like a little child in its mother's arms,
    like a little child, so I keep myself.
3 Let Israel hope in Yahweh
    henceforth and for ever.

PSALM 132

FOR THE ANNIVERSARY OF THE TRANSFER OF THE ARK

Song of Ascents

1 Yahweh, remember David
  and all the hardships he endured,
2 the oath he swore to Yahweh,
  his vow to the Mighty One of Jacob:

3 'I will not enter tent or house,
  will not climb into bed,

⁴ will not allow myself to sleep,
   not even to close my eyes,
⁵ till I have found a place for Yahweh,
   a dwelling for the Mighty One of Jacob!'

⁶ Listen, we heard of it in Ephrathah,
   we found it at Forest-Fields.
⁷ Let us go into his dwelling-place,
   and worship at his footstool.

⁸ Go up, Yahweh, to your resting-place,
   you and the ark of your strength.
⁹ Your priests are robed in saving justice,
   your faithful are shouting for joy.
¹⁰ For the sake of your servant David,
   do not reject your anointed.

¹¹ Yahweh has sworn to David,
   and will always remain true to his word,
   'I promise that I will set
   a son of yours upon your throne.
¹² If your sons observe my covenant
   and the instructions I have taught them,
   their sons too for evermore
   will occupy your throne.'

¹³ For Yahweh has chosen Zion,
   he has desired it as a home.

¹⁴ 'Here shall I rest for evermore,
here shall I make my home as I have wished.

¹⁵ 'I shall generously bless her produce,
give her needy their fill of food,
¹⁶ I shall clothe her priests with salvation,
and her faithful will sing aloud for joy.

¹⁷ 'There I shall raise up a line of descendants for David,
light a lamp for my anointed;
¹⁸ I shall clothe his enemies with shame,
while his own crown shall flourish.'

PSALM 133

BROTHERLY LOVE

Song of Ascents

¹ How good, how delightful it is
to live as brothers all together!

² It is like a fine oil on the head,
running down the beard,
running down Aaron's beard,
onto the collar of his robes.

³ It is like the dew of Hermon
falling on the heights of Zion;

for there Yahweh bestows his blessing,
everlasting life.

PSALM 134

FOR THE EVENING LITURGY

Song of Ascents

1 Come, bless Yahweh,
all you who serve Yahweh,
serving in the house of Yahweh,
in the courts of the house of our God.
Through the night watches
2 stretch out your hands towards the sanctuary
and bless Yahweh.

3 May Yahweh bless you from Zion,
he who made heaven and earth!

PSALM 135

HYMN OF PRAISE

1 Alleluia!

Praise the name of Yahweh,
you who serve Yahweh, praise him,

² serving in the house of Yahweh,
in the courts of the house of our God.

³ Praise Yahweh, for Yahweh is good,
make music for his name—it brings joy—
⁴ for Yahweh has chosen Jacob for himself,
Israel as his own possession.

⁵ For I know that Yahweh is great,
our Lord is above all gods.
⁶ Yahweh does whatever he pleases
in heaven, on earth,
in the waters and all the depths.

⁷ He summons up clouds from the borders of earth,
sends rain with lightning-flashes,
and brings the wind out of his storehouse.

⁸ He struck the first-born in Egypt,
man and beast alike,
⁹ he sent signs and wonders into the heart of Egypt,
against Pharaoh and all his officials.

¹⁰ He struck down many nations,
he slaughtered mighty kings,
¹¹ Sihon king of the Amorites,
and Og king of Bashan,
and all the kingdoms of Canaan.

¹² He gave their land as a birthright,
a birthright to his people Israel.

¹³ Yahweh, your name endures for ever,
Yahweh, your memory is fresh from age to age.
¹⁴ For Yahweh vindicates his people,
feels compassion for his servants.

¹⁵ The idols of the nations are silver and gold,
made by human hands.
¹⁶ These have mouths but say nothing,
have eyes but see nothing,

¹⁷ have ears but hear nothing,
and they have no breath in their mouths.
¹⁸ Their makers will end up like them,
everyone who relies on them.

¹⁹ House of Israel, bless Yahweh,
House of Aaron, bless Yahweh,
²⁰ House of Levi, bless Yahweh,
you who fear Yahweh, bless Yahweh.

²¹ Blessed be Yahweh from Zion,
he who dwells in Jerusalem!

PSALM 136

LITANY OF THANKSGIVING

Alleluia!

1 Give thanks to Yahweh for he is good,
for his faithful love endures for ever.
2 Give thanks to the God of gods,
for his faithful love endures for ever.
3 Give thanks to the Lord of lords,
for his faithful love endures for ever.

4 He alone works wonders,
for his faithful love endures for ever.
5 In wisdom he made the heavens,
for his faithful love endures for ever.
6 He set the earth firm on the waters,
for his faithful love endures for ever.

7 He made the great lights,
for his faithful love endures for ever.
8 The sun to rule the day,
for his faithful love endures for ever.
9 Moon and stars to rule the night,
for his faithful love endures for ever.

10 He struck down the first-born of Egypt,
for his faithful love endures for ever.

¹¹ He brought Israel out from among them,
  for his faithful love endures for ever.
¹² With mighty hand and outstretched arm,
  for his faithful love endures for ever.

¹³ He split the Sea of Reeds in two,
  for his faithful love endures for ever.
¹⁴ Let Israel pass through the middle,
  for his faithful love endures for ever.
¹⁵ And drowned Pharaoh and all his army,
  for his faithful love endures for ever.

¹⁶ He led his people through the desert,
  for his faithful love endures for ever.
¹⁷ He struck down mighty kings,
  for his faithful love endures for ever.
¹⁸ Slaughtered famous kings,
  for his faithful love endures for ever.
¹⁹ Sihon king of the Amorites,
  for his faithful love endures for ever.
²⁰ And Og king of Bashan,
  for his faithful love endures for ever.

²¹ He gave their land as a birthright,
  for his faithful love endures for ever.
²² A birthright to his servant Israel,
  for his faithful love endures for ever.
²³ He kept us in mind when we were humbled,

for his faithful love endures for ever.
²⁴ And rescued us from our enemies,
for his faithful love endures for ever.

²⁵ He provides food for all living creatures,
for his faithful love endures for ever.
²⁶ Give thanks to the God of heaven,
for his faithful love endures for ever.

PSALM 137

SONG OF THE EXILES

¹ By the rivers of Babylon
we sat and wept
at the memory of Zion.
² On the poplars there
we had hung up our harps.

³ For there our gaolers had asked us
to sing them a song,
our captors to make merry,
'Sing us one of the songs of Zion.'

⁴ How could we sing a song of Yahweh
on alien soil?
⁵ If I forget you, Jerusalem,
may my right hand wither!

6 May my tongue remain stuck to my palate
    if I do not keep you in mind,
    if I do not count Jerusalem
    the greatest of my joys.

7 Remember, Yahweh, to the Edomites' cost,
    the day of Jerusalem,
    how they said, 'Down with it! Rase it to the ground!'

8 Daughter of Babel, doomed to destruction,
    a blessing on anyone
    who treats you as you treated us,
9 a blessing on anyone who seizes your babies
    and shatters them against a rock!

PSALM 138

HYMN OF THANKSGIVING

Of David

1 I thank you, Yahweh, with all my heart,
    for you have listened to the cry I uttered.
    In the presence of angels I sing to you,
2 I bow down before your holy Temple.

    I praise your name for your faithful love and your
        constancy;
    your promises surpass even your fame.

³ You heard me on the day when I called,
and you gave new strength to my heart.

⁴ All the kings of the earth give thanks to you, Yahweh,
when they hear the promises you make;
⁵ they sing of Yahweh's ways,
' Great is the glory of Yahweh!'
⁶ Sublime as he is, Yahweh looks on the humble,
the proud he picks out from afar.

⁷ Though I live surrounded by trouble
you give me life—to my enemies' fury!
You stretch out your right hand and save me,
⁸ Yahweh will do all things for me.
Yahweh, your faithful love endures for ever,
do not abandon what you have made.

PSALM 139

IN PRAISE OF GOD'S OMNISCIENCE

For the choirmaster   Of David   Psalm

¹ Yahweh, you examine me and know me,
² you know when I sit, when I rise,
you understand my thoughts from afar.
³ You watch when I walk or lie down,
you know every detail of my conduct.

⁴ A word is not yet on my tongue
  before you, Yahweh, know all about it.
⁵ You fence me in, behind and in front,
  you have laid your hand upon me.
⁶ Such amazing knowledge is beyond me,
  a height to which I cannot attain.

⁷ Where shall I go to escape your spirit?
  Where shall I flee from your presence?
⁸ If I scale the heavens you are there,
  if I lie flat in Sheol, there you are.

⁹ If I speed away on the wings of the dawn,
  if I dwell beyond the ocean,
¹⁰ even there your hand will be guiding me,
  your right hand holding me fast.

¹¹ I will say, 'Let the darkness cover me,
  and the night wrap itself around me,'
¹² even darkness to you is not dark,
  and night is as clear as the day.

¹³ You created my inmost self,
  knit me together in my mother's womb.
¹⁴ For so many marvels I thank you;
  a wonder am I, and all your works are wonders.

  You knew me through and through,

¹⁵ my being held no secrets from you,
   when I was being formed in secret,
   textured in the depths of the earth.

¹⁶ Your eyes could see my embryo.
   In your book all my days were inscribed,
   every one that was fixed is there.

¹⁷ How hard for me to grasp your thoughts,
   how many, God, there are!
¹⁸ If I count them, they are more than the grains of sand;
   if I come to an end, I am still with you.

¹⁹ If only, God, you would kill the wicked!—
   Men of violence, keep away from me!—
²⁰ those who speak blasphemously about you,
   and take no account of your thoughts.

²¹ Yahweh, do I not hate those who hate you,
   and loathe those who defy you?
²² My hate for them has no limits,
   I regard them as my own enemies.

²³ God, examine me and know my heart,
   test me and know my concerns.
²⁴ Make sure that I am not on my way to ruin,
   and guide me on the road of eternity.

PSALM 140

AGAINST THE WICKED

For the choirmaster   Psalm   Of David

¹ Rescue me, Yahweh, from evil men,
   protect me from violent men,
² whose heart is bent on malice,
   day after day they harbour strife;
³ their tongues as barbed as a serpent's,
   viper's venom behind their lips.   *Pause*

⁴ Keep me, Yahweh, from the clutches of the wicked,
   protect me from violent men,
who are bent on making me stumble,
   ^{5a} laying out snares where I walk,
^{5a} in their arrogance hiding pitfall and noose
   ^{5c} to trap me as I pass.   *Pause*

⁶ I said to Yahweh, 'You are my God.'
   Listen, Yahweh, to the sound of my prayer.
⁷ Yahweh my Lord, my saving strength,
   you shield my head when battle comes.
⁸ Yahweh, do not grant the wicked their wishes,
   do not let their plots succeed.   *Pause*

Do not let my attackers ⁹prevail,
   but let them be overwhelmed by their own malice.

¹⁰ May red-hot embers rain down on them,
  may they be flung into the mire once and for all.
¹¹ May the slanderer find no rest anywhere,
  may evil hunt down violent men implacably.

¹² I know that Yahweh will give judgement for the wretched,
  justice for the needy.
¹³ The upright shall praise your name,
  the honest dwell in your presence.

PSALM 141

AGAINST THE ATTRACTIONS OF EVIL

Psalm   Of David

¹ Yahweh, I am calling, hurry to me,
  listen to my voice when I call to you.
² May my prayer be like incense in your presence,
  my uplifted hands like the evening sacrifice.

³ Yahweh, mount a guard over my mouth,
  a guard at the door of my lips.
⁴ Check any impulse to speak evil,
  to share the foul deeds of evil-doers.

  I shall not sample their delights!
⁵ May the upright correct me with a friend's rebuke;

but the wicked shall never anoint my head with oil,
for that would make me party to their crimes.

6 They are delivered into the power of the rock, their
    judge,
   those who took pleasure in hearing me say,
7 'Like a shattered millstone on the ground
   our bones are scattered at the mouth of Sheol.'

8 To you, Yahweh, I turn my eyes,
   in you I take refuge, do not leave me unprotected.
9 Save me from the traps that are set for me,
   the snares of evil-doers.

10 Let the wicked fall each into his own net,
     while I pass on my way.

PSALM 142

PRAYER IN PERSECUTION

Psalm   Of David   When he was in the cave   Prayer

1 To Yahweh I cry out with my plea.
T o Yahweh I cry out with entreaty.
2 I pour out my worry in his presence,
   in his presence I unfold my troubles.
3 However faint my spirit;
   you are watching over my path.

On the road I have to travel
they have hidden a trap for me.

⁴ Look on my right and see—
there is no one who recognises me.
All refuge is denied me,
no one cares whether I live or die.

⁵ I cry out to you, Yahweh,
I affirm, 'You are my refuge,
my share in the land of the living!'
⁶ Listen to my calling,
for I am miserably weak.

Rescue me from my persecutors,
for they are too strong for me.
⁷ Lead me out of prison
that I may praise your name.
The upright gather round me
because of your generosity to me.

PSALM 143

A HUMBLE ENTREATY

Psalm   Of David

¹ Yahweh, hear my prayer,
listen to my pleading;
in your constancy answer me,

in your saving justice;
² do not put your servant on trial,
    for no one living can be found guiltless at your tribunal.

³ An enemy is in deadly pursuit,
    crushing me into the ground,
    forcing me to live in darkness,
    like those long dead.
⁴ My spirit is faint,
    and within me my heart is numb with fear.

⁵ I recall the days of old,
    reflecting on all your deeds,
    I ponder the works of your hands.
⁶ I stretch out my hands to you,
    my heart like a land thirsty for you.   *Pause*

⁷ Answer me quickly, Yahweh,
    my spirit is worn out;
    do not turn away your face from me,
    or I shall be like those who sink into oblivion.

⁸ Let dawn bring news of your faithful love,
    for I place my trust in you;
    show me the road I must travel
    for you to relieve my heart.

⁹ Rescue me from my enemies, Yahweh,

since in you I find protection.
¹⁰ Teach me to do your will,
for you are my God.
May your generous spirit lead me
on even ground.

¹¹ Yahweh, for the sake of your name,
in your saving justice give me life,
rescue me from distress.
¹² In your faithful love annihilate my enemies,
destroy all those who oppress me,
for I am your servant.

PSALM 144

HYMN FOR WAR AND VICTORY

Of David

¹ Blessed be Yahweh, my rock,
who trains my hands for war
and my fingers for battle,
² my faithful love, my bastion,
my citadel, my Saviour;
I shelter behind him, my shield,
he makes the peoples submit to me.

³ Yahweh, what is a human being for you to notice,
a child of Adam for you to think about?

⁴ Human life, a mere puff of wind,
   days as fleeting as a shadow.

⁵ Yahweh, part the heavens and come down,
   touch the mountains, make them smoke.
⁶ Scatter them with continuous lightning-flashes,
   rout them with a volley of your arrows.

⁷ Stretch down your hand from above,
   save me, rescue me from deep waters,
   from the clutches of foreigners,
⁸ whose every word is worthless,
   whose right hand is raised in perjury.

⁹ God, I sing to you a new song,
   I play to you on the ten-stringed lyre,
¹⁰ for you give kings their victories,
   you rescue your servant David.

From the sword of evil ¹¹save me,
   rescue me from the clutches of foreigners
   whose every word is worthless,
   whose right hand testifies to falsehood.

¹² May our sons be like plants
      growing tall from their earliest days,
   our daughters like pillars
      carved fit for a palace,

¹³ our barns filled to overflowing
   with every kind of crop,
the sheep in our pastures be numbered
   in thousands and tens of thousands,

¹⁴ our cattle well fed,
   free of raids and pillage,
   free of outcry in our streets.

¹⁵ How blessed the nation of whom this is true,
   blessed the nation whose God is Yahweh!

PSALM 145

PRAISE TO YAHWEH THE KING

Hymn of Praise   Of David

Aleph ¹ I shall praise you to the heights, God my King,
            I shall bless your name for ever and ever.
Bet   ² Day after day I shall bless you,
            I shall praise your name for ever and ever.
Gimel ³ Great is Yahweh and worthy of all praise,
            his greatness beyond all reckoning.

Dalet ⁴ Each age will praise your deeds to the next,
            proclaiming your mighty works.
He   ⁵ Your renown is the splendour of your glory,
            I will ponder the story of your wonders.

Waw   ⁶ They will speak of your awesome power,
      and I shall recount your greatness.

Zain   ⁷ They will bring out the memory of your great
         generosity,
      and joyfully acclaim your saving justice.

Het   ⁸ Yahweh is tenderness and pity,
      slow to anger, full of faithful love.

Tet   ⁹ Yahweh is generous to all,
      his tenderness embraces all his creatures.

Yod   ¹⁰ All your creatures shall thank you, Yahweh,
      and your faithful shall bless you.

Kaph   ¹¹ They shall speak of the glory of your kingship
      and tell of your might,

Lamed ¹² making known your mighty deeds to the
         children of Adam,
      the glory and majesty of your kingship.

Mem   ¹³ Your kingship is a kingship for ever,
      your reign lasts from age to age.

(Nun)   Yahweh is trustworthy in all his words,
      and upright in all his deeds.

Samek ¹⁴ Yahweh supports all who stumble,
      lifts up those who are bowed down.

Ain   ¹⁵ All look to you in hope

and you feed them with the food of the season.

Pe ¹⁶ And, with generous hand,
you satisfy the desires of every living creature.

Zade ¹⁷ Upright in all that he does,
Yahweh acts only in faithful love.

Qoph ¹⁸ He is close to all who call upon him,
all who call on him from the heart.

Resh ¹⁹ He fulfils the desires of all who fear him,
he hears their cry and he saves them.

Shin ²⁰ Yahweh guards all who love him,
but all the wicked he destroys.

Taw ²¹ My mouth shall always praise Yahweh,
let every creature bless his holy name
for ever and ever.

PSALM 146

HYMN TO THE GOD OF HELP

¹ Alleluia!
Praise Yahweh, my soul!
² I will praise Yahweh all my life,
I will make music to my God as long as I live.

³ Do not put your trust in princes,
in any child of Adam, who has no power to save.

⁴ When his spirit goes forth he returns to the earth,
   on that very day all his plans come to nothing.

⁵ How blessed is he who has Jacob's God to help him,
   his hope is in Yahweh his God,
⁶ who made heaven and earth,
   the sea and all that is in them.

   He keeps faith for ever,
⁷ gives justice to the oppressed,
   gives food to the hungry;
   Yahweh sets prisoners free.

⁸ Yahweh gives sight to the blind,
   lifts up those who are bowed down.
⁹ Yahweh protects the stranger,
   he sustains the orphan and the widow.

⁸ᶜ Yahweh loves the upright,
⁹ᶜ but he frustrates the wicked.
¹⁰ Yahweh reigns for ever,
   your God, Zion, from age to age.

PSALM 147

HYMN TO THE ALL-POWERFUL

   Alleluia!

¹ Praise Yahweh—it is good to sing psalms

to our God—how pleasant to praise him.
² Yahweh, Builder of Jerusalem!
  He gathers together the exiles of Israel,
³ healing the broken-hearted
  and binding up their wounds;
⁴ he counts out the number of the stars,
  and gives each one of them a name.

⁵ Our Lord is great, all-powerful,
  his wisdom beyond all telling.
⁶ Yahweh sustains the poor,
  and humbles the wicked to the ground.

⁷ Sing to Yahweh in thanksgiving,
  play the harp for our God.
⁸ He veils the sky with clouds,
  and provides the earth with rain,
  makes grass grow on the hills
  and plants for people to use,
⁹ gives fodder to cattle
  and to young ravens when they cry.

¹⁰ He takes no delight in the power of horses,
  no pleasure in human sturdiness;
¹¹ his pleasure is in those who fear him,
  in those who hope in his faithful love.

¹² Praise Yahweh, Jerusalem,
  Zion, praise your God.

¹³ For he gives strength to the bars of your gates,
   he blesses your children within you,
¹⁴ he maintains the peace of your frontiers,
   gives you your fill of finest wheat.

¹⁵ He sends his word to the earth,
   his command runs quickly,
¹⁶ he spreads the snow like flax,
   strews hoarfrost like ashes,

¹⁷ he sends ice-crystals like breadcrumbs,
   and who can withstand that cold?
¹⁸ When he sends his word it thaws them,
   when he makes his wind blow, the waters are unstopped.

¹⁹ He reveals his word to Jacob,
   his statutes and judgements to Israel.
²⁰ For no other nation has he done this,
   no other has known his judgements.

PSALM 148

COSMIC HYMN OF PRAISE

¹ Alleluia!

Praise Yahweh from the heavens,
praise him in the heights.

² Praise him, all his angels,
  praise him, all his host!

³ Praise him, sun and moon,
  praise him, all shining stars,
⁴ praise him, highest heavens,
  praise him, waters above the heavens.

⁵ Let them praise the name of Yahweh
  at whose command they were made;
⁶ he established them for ever and ever
  by an unchanging decree.

⁷ Praise Yahweh from the earth,
  sea-monsters and all the depths,
⁸ fire and hail, snow and mist,
  storm-winds that obey his word,

⁹ mountains and every hill,
  orchards and every cedar,
¹⁰ wild animals and all cattle,
  reptiles and winged birds,

¹¹ kings of the earth and all nations,
  princes and all judges on earth,
¹² young men and girls,
  old people and children together.

¹³ Let them praise the name of Yahweh,
for his name alone is sublime,
his splendour transcends earth and heaven.
¹⁴ For he heightens the strength of his people,
to the praise of all his faithful,
the children of Israel, the people close to him.

PSALM 149

SONG OF TRIUMPH

¹ Alleluia!

Sing a new song to Yahweh:
his praise in the assembly of the faithful!
² Israel shall rejoice in its Maker,
the children of Zion delight in their king;
³ they shall dance in praise of his name,
play to him on tambourines and harp!

⁴ For Yahweh loves his people,
he will crown the humble with salvation.
⁵ The faithful exult in glory,
shout for joy as they worship him,
⁶ praising God to the heights with their voices,
a two-edged sword in their hands,

⁷ to wreak vengeance on the nations,
punishment on the peoples,

8 to load their kings with chains
   and their nobles with iron fetters,
9 to execute on them the judgement passed—
   to the honour of all his faithful.

PSALM 150

FINAL CHORUS OF PRAISE

1 Alleluia!

   Praise God in his holy place,
   praise him in the heavenly vault of his power,
2 praise him for his mighty deeds,
   praise him for all his greatness.

3 Praise him with fanfare of trumpet,
   praise him with harp and lyre,
4 praise him with tambourines and dancing,
   praise him with strings and pipes,
5 praise him with the clamour of cymbals,
   praise him with triumphant cymbals,
6 Let everything that breathes praise Yahweh.

   Alleluia!